Outdoors
Scotland

Pat Gerber

a guide to enjoying the great Scottish countryside

Argyll
publishing

For Bryony, with love

© text and photos
Pat Gerber 2000

First published 2000
Argyll Publishing
Glendaruel
Argyll PA22 3AE
Scotland

The author has asserted her moral rights.

British Library Cataloguing-in-Publication Data.
A catalogue record for this book is available from the British Library.

ISBN 1 902831 13 6

Cover photo
Andrew Morris

Origination
Cordfall Ltd, Glasgow

Printing
ColourBooks, Dublin

Acknowledgements
THANKS are due to the YMCA for their generous support in bringing this book into print.

Many people and organisations have given generously of their time and expertise to help in its preparation. In particular I would like to thank David Barclay, Andy and Laura Bowden, the Carnie family, Ally Corbett, Kate Cuthbert, Bridget Dales, Margot Delaney, George Duff, John Easton, Malcolm Fife, Cyril Gerber, Bill Harte, Carol Huston, Alison Irvine, Mary Legge, Janice Lindsay, Jennifer Macleod, Elidh-Ann Madden, Greg and Grace Morris, Mark Palmer, Davy Paterson, Ali Paton, Peter Pearson, John Phillips, Bob Reid, Derek Rodger, Helen Rowbotham, Dallas Seawright, Duncan Stevenson, Andy Summers, Blair Wilkie and Alison Wilson.

Pat Gerber
Glasgow
March 2000

Foreword

WHAT do you think you are doing? Yes YOU. How long are you intending to sit in that armchair surrounded by the same four walls and stare at that TV screen? What has happened to your sense of adventure, your free spirit? Isn't it about time you ventured outside into the unknown? Explored what Scotland has to offer? Allowed your body and mind to roam free in the great big world beyond your front door?

Ali Paton

Scotland is brimming over with fantastic scenery, interesting places and wonderful wildlife. You don't have to be an experienced explorer or first class mountaineer to sample these treasures. You certainly don't need to wear a crash helmet. All you need is the desire to leave the confines of city life and go in search of freedom. Discover the other side of Scotland – the side that will leave you feeling liberated and alive. So go on, turn the pages of this inviting book and go . . . you never know what you might discover about Scotland . . . or yourself.   *Ali Paton*

THIS exciting and informative book will appeal to a wide range of ordinary people like myself who are interested in exploring in a leisurely way the intrinsic beauty and places of interest which abound in Scotland. Aimed at individuals, friends and families, *Outdoors Scotland* presents an array of opportunities that require no expensive equipment or costly entrance fees, but simply the enthusiasm that can lead to new discoveries and experiences.

YMCA Glasgow is delighted to be associated with this publication. Working primarily with disadvantaged and vulnerable people, whether young people at risk on our streets, homeless people or asylum seekers from less peaceful parts of the world, we recognise the value of the kind of readily accessible experiences described here. These are one important means towards helping all of us to rediscover ourselves and our values in the positive and healthy environment of countryside and seascape, and in the company of fellow adventurers. Thank you for supporting the work of YMCA Glasgow.   *Bill Harte*, Chief Exec.

The Great Scottish Outdoors

NEARLY everyone in Scotland now lives in a town, where everything we need is provided; places for work, study and entertainment. Everything, that is, except fresh air, freedom and adventure.

Freedom is Out There

Out-of-town can feel like 'keep-off' territory. No wonder we prefer a comfy urban couch to landscapes bristling with stalkers, grouse-shooters and fierce dogs. Fields full of sheep and mad bulls are fenced with live wires.

But there ARE places, till now known only by locals, where we can help ourselves to the airy freedoms of Scotland, where we ARE welcome to roam safely with our children, where we CAN go out to play whatever our age and state of ability. People-friendly outdoor areas now, at the beginning of the new millennium, include National Scenic Areas, National Parks, Regional Parks, Country Parks, Countryside Around Town Projects, Forest Enterprise areas, parts of RSPB reserves, other Nature Reserves, Rights of Way, various Footpath initiatives, Long Distance Routes, several river valley projects, canal towpaths, horse-riding trails and Sustrans' cycle-paths. There are also open gardens around some NTS and Historic Scotland properties and many lovely little private estates.

A common factor is usually a welcoming notice or way-marking post, however small. These give us the confidence that there will be walkable paths, stiles to help us over walls and fences, and gates we can easily open and shut.

Beyond the Streetlight Zone

Scotland is an amazing country. We're packed so tightly together in our towns that most of Scotland is landscape, much of it classified as a great European wilderness. Wolves and bears may no longer stalk us, but anyone can learn how to track the existing, less-threatening, wildlife here. We have every kind of terrain, from huge mountains to squelching blanket-bog, every sort of water from big river to canal and loch. We have shorelines of all sorts from fearsome cliffs to beaches smooth as peach-skin. And we can experience every sort of weather,

from the warm airs of the North Atlantic Drift to Arctic blizzards howling across the Grampians.

Help

How can we find out how to access all of this? One of the most pleasurable ways to experience either a new place or a new activity is in the company of one of Scotland's Countryside Rangers. These friendly, down-to-earth experts make it their business to understand their territory, its wildlife, plants – and its potential for interesting recreation. One of their work functions is to share both their specialist knowledge and their local insights with us. Ever thought of taking part in a Walking Festival? Know where to buy a fishing permit for £12 on one Scotland's greatest rivers? Fancy lambing? Tried making nettle soup and wondered – er – why?

How Do You Know?

Sometimes with the help of Countryside Rangers and sometimes alone, the author travelled the Scottish mainland looking for accessible places where everyone is welcome. On her journey she interviewed a wide variety of people, from picnicking Scots families to wandering travellers from all over the world. No-one has paid in any way to be included in this guide and all the opinions expressed are her own. Being human, and therefore fallible, she will have missed things. You are cordially invited to put her right; please feel free to write in about your own favourite places, your experiences good and bad around the Scottish countryside, and any opinions you care to share.

Read and Go!

First, take a look at what follows. The book is organised in six sections; Highlands, North-east, Heart of Scotland, Glasgow and the West, Edinburgh and the Lothians, Borders and the South. It takes a good look at the countryside that's accessible to all of us right now. Reading through, or dipping in, you might be alerted to new facilities, be inspired to try new experiences, be introduced to people you knew nothing about till now, or be incited to revisit scenes from your past. But, most of all, this guide aims to help you find bits of Scotland – and maybe even bits of yourself – you never dreamed of.

Scottish Countryside Rangers

TO TRAVEL a few miles of Scotland in the company of the Countryside Ranger who lives and works there is to gain a privileged insight that is simply not available to the casual visitor. Fully-fledged Rangers get to know their territory intimately by regularly patrolling, surveying trees and plants and observing wildlife. They lead informative guided walks, and anyone is welcome to approach them for friendly advice. They act as expert interfaces between us and Nature.

Fitter than most of us, they may also be required to chase vandals – or errant cows. They're expected to pick up – and dispose of safely – even the most revolting litter. Many of their guided walks cost nothing, some a pound or two. And they manage and carry out practical conservation work with volunteers.

The evolution of Scotland's Countryside Ranger service began in 1967 with the legislation to provide for better enjoyment of the countryside, improved access for us all, and the creation of Country Parks. Lands coming into the care of various organisations opened for recreation. Now, local authorities co-operate with bodies such as Scottish Natural Heritage, National Trust for Scotland, the Forestry Commission, Scottish Wildlife Trust and the RSPB to make more land accessible. Specialist groups such as the British Horse Society, Sustrans, the Footpath Trust and Access for All work

Canal societies are opening old towpaths and waterways for public use.

If you're used to busy town streets, big empty spaces can feel threatening. Way-marked paths and the presence of a Ranger make one feel welcome and safe. There's someone to ask, someone who knows about everything from the wildlife to the best picnic spot

to create growing networks of rides, cycle-ways and footpaths.

In Scotland, most openly accessible areas are looked after by teams of Countryside Rangers employed by local authorities, small heritage foundations, private estates and Historic Scotland. Forest Enterprise have Wildlife Rangers and Recreation Rangers, while NTS employs Ranger/ Naturalists.

photo: Andrew Morris

Skye, Loch nam Nuamh

The **HIGHLANDS**

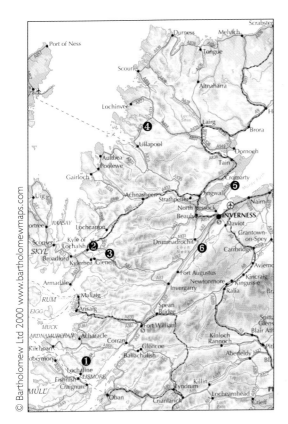

1. Ardtornish Estate
2. Plockton
3. Morvich Centre, Kintail
4. Knockan
5. South Suter Viewpoint
6. Foyers and Inverfarigaig

© Bartholomew Ltd 2000 www.bartholomewmaps.com

INFORMATION

OS Map Nos 9, 10, 11, 12, 15, 16, 17, 19, 20, 21, 23 – 27, 32 – 34, 39, 40, 47 – 49

LOCAL AUTHORITIES

Eilean Siar, Comhairle nan (previously known as Western Isles Council), Sandwick Road, Stornoway, ISLE OF LEWIS HS1 2BW Tel 01851 703773

Highland Council, Glenurquhart Road, Inverness IV3 5NX
Tel 01463 702000

Moray Council, Council Office, High Street, Elgin, Moray IV30 1BX
Tel 01343 543451

TOURIST INFORMATION CENTRES

INVERNESS Castle Wynd Inverness IV2 3BJ 01463 234353

NAIRN 62 King Street Nairn IV12 4DN Tel 01667 452753

FORT AUGUSTUS
Tel 01320 366367

KYLE OF LOCHALSH
Tel 01599 534276

PORTREE
Tel 01478 612137

WICK Tel 01955 602596

STRONTIAN Tel 01967 402131

KILCHOAN Tel 01972 510222

Website for Ardnamurchan
www.ardnamurchan.com

OTHER USEFUL ORGANISATIONS

British Waterways Regional Office
Tel 0141 332 6936

The Caledonian Canal Heritage Centre, Fort Augustus
Tel 01320 366 493

CENTRES OF INTEREST WITH COUNTRYSIDE RANGERS

DORNOCH Forest enterprise
Tel 01862 810359

DUNNET BAY North Caithness Rangers Tel 01847 821531

North of Scotland's Great Glen lies some of the world's most intriguing landscape, quite different from anywhere else in Europe. Small, widely scattered communities of resourceful inhabitants know how to enjoy themselves, and they provide plenty for visitors.

The Highland Walking Festival happens every May, with a varied programme of daytime and evening events all over the area, geared to different interests, levels of experience and fitness. All summer long, Highland Games

WICK Caithness East Rangers
Tel 01955 607758

DUNBEATH Dunbeath
Heritage Centre (Seasonal)
Tel 01593 731233

Laidhay Croft Museum,
Dunbeath Tel 01593 731244

DURNESS (includes Cape
Wrath, Smoo Cave, Scourie)
Durness Visitor Centre Ranger
Service/Tourist Information
Tel 01971 511259

LOCHINVER (includes
Clachtoll, Achmelvich, Stoer,
Drumbeg, Assynt, Kylescu)
Tel 01463 703513

LAIRG
Ranger for mid Sutherland
Tel 01549 402638

INVERNESS/NAIRN
(Coastal areas including
Cromarty, Rosemarkie,
Ardersier) Coastal Rangers
Tel 01463 724312

INVERNESS/GREAT GLEN
Countryside Rangers
Tel 01463 724260

INVERINATE (NTS)
Kintail and West Affric
Countryside Centre at Morvich
Farm Tel 01599 511231

LOCHALSH HOUSE (NTS)
Tel 01599 566325

Skye and Lochalsh Ranger
Tel 01478 813808

Skye and Lochalsh Tourist
Guides, Isle of Skye
Tel 01470 542484

LOCHMADDY RANGER
SERVICE, North Uist
Tel 01876 500829

ARDNAMURCHAN (incl
Ardnamurchan point, Portuaik,
Achnaha, Polloch, Strontian,
Ariundle, Kilchoan,
Glenborrodale, Salen, Camus
Nan Geall, Bay MacNeil)
Strontian/Ardnamurchan Ranger
Tel 01967 402232

Ardnamurchan Lighthouse Trust
(seasonal) Tel 01972 510210

Ardnamurchan Natural History
Centre Tel 01972 500209/
500254

and Gatherings showcase traditional dance, music and sport, along with events in which visitors can compete. They're also made welcome at village ceilidhs, where the age-groups mix, kids don't have to be baby-sat, the music's great and the oldies know all the steps. One of the best ideas is the summer Feis (pronounced 'faish'), where children learn traditional music and drama taught by expert performers.

Highland Scotland is brilliant for outdoor activities. Over 200,000 people arrive annually to explore hundreds of miles of accessible footpaths, yet you might never see another soul, the landscape is so big and wide. In Sutherland, mountains thrust skywards sculpted by weather into unearthly shapes coloured black or startling crystalline white. Strange rock-shapes erupt from sodden wastes of seemingly featureless bog. The sea pushes inland on the west, scooping out lochs edged with rockpools and empty beaches and, to the east, Caithness appears to have risen from the ocean like a giant scone, surrounded by impregnable cliffs.

All around the area there are Countryside Ranger bases. Highland Council's Head Ranger works from Inverness, masterminding services in visitor centres at Ardnamurchan, Lochinver, Durness, Dunnett Bay, Wick and Lairg. As to the islands of the west, Skye has a good Ranger service based at Portree; Lewis has one at Stornoway and there's one on Uist. The National Trust employ Rangers at Torridon, Knockan and Ben Eighe Nature Reserves, and Forest Enterprise, whose Head Ranger operates from Dornoch, has a team of nine Rangers spread between Bettyhill, Lybster, Lairg, and Ardross. If you prefer to travel alone, many of the paths are way-marked, with maps and information panels at junctions or points of interest, designed to be discreet enough to ignore.

There are things to be aware of in such remote regions. Midges are the most trivial, annoying between June and September on muggy days, or around boggy ground or sea-weedy shores. Clegs land silently on your skin when you're not looking, then bite you painfully. They're at their worst on moorland in August. So arm yourself with insect repellent plus an antidote to stings and bites, and cover up when necessary. Midge-nets for your head look strange, but work – and are surely better than being covered in angry red blotches? You can buy them from fishing shops and some tourist outlets. Maybe one day they'll become a fashion item, but meantime the colour choice is khaki or khaki.

Slightly more dangerous, adders are the only true snakes in Scotland. Asleep in winter, they liven up when the sun begins to warm their cold blood. They're unlikely to attack you unless they're surprised or feel threatened. But it's sensible to wear boots if you're heather-hopping in summer.

The Highlands may be remote but they're popular, so make sure you have somewhere to stay. Being benighted in Ullapool without a tent in pouring rain is not amusing

ARDTORNISH Estate Office
Tel 01967 421288
Keeper's Office
Tel 01967 421229
Forest Enterprise LOCHABER
FOREST Tel 01397 702184

TORRIDON (Seasonal)
Countryside Centre
Tel 01445 791221

PUBLIC TRANSPORT

INVERNESS AIRPORT
Tel 01463 232 471
British Airways at Inverness
Tel 01667 462 280
Easyjet Tel 0870 600 0000

SCOTRAIL Tel 0845 748 4950

BUSES
Citylink Tel 0141 332 9644
National Express Tel 0990 808080
Cape Wrath Minibus Tel 01971 511287

BOATS AND FERRIES
John O'Groats Ferries Tel 01955 611 353

In good weather, there's sometimes day-time dancing in the streets . . . of Plockton

– especially when the nearest bed is 45 miles away in the direction you've just come from. Camp sites exist near communities, but ask permission if you want to pitch your tent in the wild. Back-packers' hostels run their own mini-buses and there are Youth Hostels but distances are long, so plan with care. You can use the Tourist Board's excellent free 'book a bed-ahead' service. Especially in July and August, book in advance.

If you're driving, maps can be misleading; the mileage may look short but on single-track roads, negotiating around caravans and tour-buses can take three times as long as on double-track roads – and be three times as exhausting. So allow extra hours for your journey – and fill up when you see a petrol station open. In the summer months book car-ferries in advance – and there are still some which won't take you anywhere on Sundays. Roads may be blissfully traffic-free in winter, but for this very reason it's wise to carry food, blankets and a thermos flask of something warming. Mobile phones are not dependable in this area and you'll have to go looking for help if you need it, so pack boots and waterproofs. If the media say don't travel because of forecast snow-falls, don't travel.

The journey's end is richly rewarding, but getting this far north is sometimes still harder than it needs to be. It's useful that trains go to Kyle of Lochalsh in the west and Wick in the east, but planes stop at Inverness or fly on over the top of you to the northern isles.

All year round, Highland scenery is wonderful in good weather. Wide, ever-changing skies, great sweeps of landscape clad with heather or snow, shimmering seascapes sometimes veiled in translucent mists and rainbows, give a matchless feeling of space and tranquillity.

Try the trail between
Polloch and Glenfinnan

ARDNAMURCHAN

Ardnamurchan is one of the best-kept secrets of the
Highlands. Along with its adjoining areas of Moidart and
Morvern, stretching from Strontian along Loch Sunart out
to the most westerly point on the British mainland, there's
enough here to fill anyone's holiday, and some of the
sunniest weather in Scotland.

On Ardnamurchan, you're free to roam, providing you
observe the Countryside Code. Cycle tracks run through
the Forest Enterprise land; try the trail between Polloch and
Glenfinnan, and another to the top of Glen Hurich. Horse-
riding is possible, but tree-felling can be dangerous so check
with Forest Enterprise where it's safe to go. Hire a boat on
Loch Sheil or Loch Sunart, arrange salmon, trout or sea
fishing. But perhaps walking is the most rewarding
activity here. Throughout history, walking was how
locals got around. Ancient paths still thread between
now-silent settlements. A community woodland
project is improving pathways for the less able,
aiming for a network throughout Lochaber.

Ardnamurchan Lighthouse,
now automatic, houses a
museum illustrating the
history of lighthouses and
their keepers, with a café and
loos and from there, on a
clear day, you can see the
Outer Hebrides and maybe
minkie whales, porpoises or
seals. In stormy weather it's
wild

A Countryside Ranger alternates her base
between Strontian (Forest Enterprise building) and
the Community Centre at Kilchoan – stop her well-
marked van if you've an enquiry. She leads walks
about local history, wildlife, archaeology and
woodland. With her you might travel backwards
through time into ancient Ariundle Oakwood,
undisturbed for centuries, see where the Sluagh an
Torraidh Bhan (people of the white hillock) slashed

Remote Glen Drian township
in its vast extinct volcano

and burned to make the ground fertile enough for crops and recognise their cottages, cleared for sheep after a villager joined the Jacobite army in 1745.

Or consider the archaeology of Cams nan Geall, remote Glen Drian township in its vast extinct volcano, Bay MacNeill hidden below the cliffs of Ardnamurchan point, or hear about the big regeneration plan for Ardnamurchan's Atlantic Oakwood.

Spend time at the Scottish Wildlife Trust reserve on Rahoy Hills, or the RSPB reserve at Glenborrodale, or try a creepy night-watch in the hideouts of bats.

Good places to visit include the unimaginatively-named but excellent Natural History Centre, for real home baking and a close encounter with the old breeds of animal – sometimes wild red deer graze on the turf roof. There's a good range of gifts and books on sale and you can explore a dark and creepy wildcat's lair in the visitor centre – if you dare. Ardtornish Estate has a good reputation for welcoming walkers.

Acharacle is a pretty village in idyllic surroundings, near Kentra Bay. In July Acharacle Week has everything from dog shows to raft racing and there's a resident Feis. Kilchoan has its Show and, in August, a model yacht picnic, and the Western Ardnamurchan Regatta. There's also Strontian's Agricultural Show and Gymkhana. Wherever you go in summer head for the local ceilidh and dance the night away.

Inverewe Gardens

SKYE AND THE WEST

Between Arisaig and Ullapool lies spectacular scenery. A deeply indented coastline dotted with pretty villages like Applecross and Plockton leads inland to the massive Torridon mountains. The Cuillins on the Isle of Skye are no less magnificent. They have inspired painters and poets, but even the crampon set fall off them regularly so most of us are best admiring them, whilst exploring everywhere else on the island.

The Skye and Lochalsh Countryside Ranger takes guided walks from April to September and runs a Watch Club for 8-12 year-old bird enthusiasts, in conjunction with his Kintail colleague.

With him you might check out woodland wildlife, meet the Old Man of Storr, feast on funghi under the Fairy Flag of Dunvegan Castle, or look at lichens on scary Neist Point while trying to concentrate on vertigo-insensitive birds. Nearby, on the island of Sandaig, seek for descendants of

If you enjoy walking or cycling among mountains, Torridon and Ben Eighe are for you

Gavin Maxwell's otter. At Glenelg, dive backwards in time 2,000 years as you explore its two Brochs. Breakfast with the birds on the Plock of Kyle, see traditional crofting at Drumbuie, look at the low-tide sea-life around the village of Plockton, location of TV's *Hamish Macbeth*.

Lochalsh Woodland Garden's Countryside Ranger organises summer events and at famous Inverewe Garden explore Wet Valley, the bay of Camas Glas, or get lost in Bambooselem with its Ranger.

The Five Sisters of Kintail are big girls, four over 3,000 ft. high. At the foot of these mountains, Morvich Countryside Centre shows walks like the old Skye-Dingwall drove road joining Kintail to Glomach and its famous Falls – further in than many folk realise, says the Ranger. She organises a programme of walks in July and August, some high level, but anytime from March to September she'll do her best to help any group that phones in advance.

Torridon, a tiny village complete with shop, loos, a campsite, has an NTS Ranger centre with audio-visual information on the local geology and wildlife. Ranger-led walks for different fitness levels happen in July and August. Aultroy, one entry point to Ben Eighe Nature Reserve, has a visitor centre with loos. On sunny days the quartzite summit of Slioch glistens like silver and you can wander paths through Caledonian forest or hillsides.

Shoreline walks are also good. You can reach the circular Wester Ross Coastal Trail, marked with a Pictish fish symbol, from Kyle of Lochalsh. Catch the rainbows en-route from

Inveralligin

Badachro to Redpoint. Walk round to the Big Sand, by Rua Reidh and Melvaig, starting from the crofting community of Aultbea, made famous in the fifties by a local girl Kay Matheson, who helped bring the Coronation Stone home to Scotland. The coastlines around Gairloch also have wonderful beaches.

Corrieshalloch Gorge, gouged out of rock by meltwater when the ice-age ended, is exciting when the River Broom's in spate. From a bouncy suspension bridge, you watch it hurtle 150 ft down the Falls of Measach.

Sandy beaches abound, empty, or with camp-sites like Achmelvich (above). Countryside Rangers organise walks along their nature trails

WESTER ROSS & SUTHERLAND

The Sutherland coast begins with fishing villages like Achiltibuie and Lochinver, but the land throws up geological marvels like Suilven and the Moine Thrust at Knockan. Ridges of wind-flayed rock interspersed with trout-filled lochs lead to silent straths, empty of the crofters who lived there till the Clearances.

Wastelands of bog blanket Cape Wrath, where gales can actually blow you over. There's a sense of violence here, of forces too powerful for mere mortals. But there's lots to do.

Watch whales, dolphins and sharks swimming close round Stoer Point. Learn how to catch wild brown-trout. Hire a mountain bike locally and go exploring. Visit the sea-bird colonies on Handa Island, or the puffins of Faraidh Head. Try sea-angling, or a wild-life cruise from Durness, Scourie, Kylescu or Ullapool.

Ullapool is a busy fishing port, the ferry terminal for the Outer Hebrides, a good tourist centre and great place for meeting people from all over the world. It's stuffed full of B&Bs, hostels, hotels and camping facilities, all of which seem permanently full. On the shingly beach at Ardmair you might find amethysts or moss agates. Or try a boat trip to the sparsely populated Summer Isles. Only wild goats now live on Horse Island – but there's supposed to be gold buried there from a Spanish galleon. You might see otters or perhaps a sea-eagle – and there's an annual sand-sculpture contest.

Visit Cape Wrath with the Durness Ranger and you'll forget the interminable queue for the passenger ferry, the nauseating half-hour mini-bus ride, the bomb-blasted buildings, the MD poison-warning signs, and the lack of even the most basic facilities such as a loo when you get there. Instead, while cross-legged tourists gaze mystified at bog-land, you'll be transported on a magic carpet of rare plants decorated with endangered butterflies and jewelled with strange insects while he decodes the archaeological and geological story of Scotland hidden amongst its peat-hags. Finally you'll be walked to a sweet little sandy bay amongst myriads of laughing sea-birds, and told their names.

There are two excellent Countryside Ranger bases – at Lochinver and (above) Durness Visitor Centre

Nature Reserves with good visitor centres include Inchnadamph and Inverpolly. Near Inchnadamph (Stag's Meadow) the Traligill and the Allt Nam Uamh burns disappear underground. Deep in creepy limestone caves here, the remains of Reindeer, Bear, Lynx and Arctic Fox were discovered, with two human skeletons from 6,000 years ago. Inverpolly has present-day wildlife and famous mountains like Stac Pollaidh.

Walk the spectacular two miles from Stoer lighthouse and see the Old Man of Stoer sticking 200 ft out of the sea. Travel the Knockan trail with its Ranger and learn about thrusts, metamorphism and intrusions of the geological kind at its visitor centre. See the cheery river Allt Smoo chortling down from Loch Meadaidh to a flower-filled dell near Durness, where it vanishes. Teeter down the dizzy cliff path, enter the gaping maw of Smoo Cave and follow a boardwalk into the darkness. Suddenly you're gazing up at the sky, fringed with those self-same flowers, the river chuckling out under your feet.

Sea birds nest on the island of Stroma near John O'Groats

CAITHNESS

The triangle of Scotland between John O'Groats, Helmsdale and Bettyhill includes the famous Flow Country. Around the coasts are white beaches, fearsome cliffs, ruined castles, brochs and Dounreay nuclear power station. Beyond, Atlantic tides storm into the North Sea through the Pentland Firth, tossing whirlpools round the jagged sea-stacks of Duncansby Head, where sea-birds dive and scream. Artists and writers find inspiration in this theatre of natural drama; the annual Northlands Festival links Scottish and Scandinavian music, stories are told of gold, pearls, blowholes – and a vanishing village. And there's lots of wildlife.

Caithness Critters, normally aged 8-12, allowed to bring the occasional adult and spade, meet twice a month all summer. They plant trees to shelter migrating birds, go on 'cliff-hanger' walks searching for puffins at Duncansby Head and spend 'batty-wicker' evenings discovering which bats hang out around Wick and how one bat can digest 3,000 midges a day. Critter trips are free (donations welcome). All age-groups can enter seashore sculpture contests and treasure hunts, marvel at blowholes blowing, or enjoy a wheelchair run along the well-designed Dunnet Forest trails to see, feel and hear clues to this woodland's story. There's an ancient dyke, a hut circle, textured barks, lichens, deer, pond-skaters, whirlygigs and damselflies. The National Cycle Network passes nearby on its way from John O'Groats to Inverness.

The Flow country is a wilderness of wetly beautiful blanket bog veined with rivers, dubh (black) lochs and silvery drifts of bog-cotton. Till rudely interrupted by tax-dodging pop-stars and their forestry schemes, these thicknesses of sphagnum moss spent six centuries creating themselves. They're now protected. Visit the RSPB visitor centre at Forsinard to discover which plants and animals love to live in bog-land.

Caithness has character. Wind-blown crushed-shell sand has created an unusual ecology at Invernaver Nature Reserve and two centuries ago the original Reay village vanished beneath tons of it. Plentiful supplies of Caithness flagstone make fields look as if they're enclosed with gravestones.

Climb the misty moors with Wick's Countryside Rangers and discuss who's buried in the creepy Grey Cairns of Camster. Less scary are their shore-shuffles, strath strolls, bat-chats (complete with bat-detectors) or marine talks for divers. See where glaciers shoved giant flagstones, discover castles stuck on vertiginous sea-stacks, or trip down memory lane to the Trinkie, a swimming pool carved from bedrock. Inland, walk up Wick River or seek the Healing Well, or the Hill of Peace near Dunbeath.

Dunbeath Water runs through 6,000 years of Scottish history between its source and the sea. It pours through a spectacular gorge, emerges near a broch hidden in a little roundel, passes an old mill, a fishing village and ends in Dunbeath harbour, still in use. This is the river made famous by Neil Gunn's (1891-1973) novel *Highland River*. He was born in Dunbeath Strath and his old school now makes a good Heritage Centre.

Bonxies and Razorbills, stoats and weasels perch, sleekly stuffed like a taxidermists' dream, in Dunnett Bay's lively Countryside Ranger centre. Identify them here, then show off your knowledge along dizzy Duncansby cliffs (note – fulmars spit smelly vomit if you get too close)

Latheron Harbour near Dunbeath

photo: Andrew Morris

Cromarty Firth

EASTER ROSS &THE BLACK ISLE

From Struie hill you get a good general view of this gentler landscape. Westward lie the broad straths of East Sutherland, watersheds of famous salmon rivers like the Oykel. Eastward, the coast splits into fertile peninsulas separated by big seaways – the Dornoch Firth, the Cromarty Firth and the Moray Firth. Here are flower-filled villages, magnificent beaches, nature reserves, whisky distilleries, Pictish stones, dolphins, the inevitable RAF target range, great golf courses – and the poshest Youth Hostel in Scotland. There are also tales of clearances, seers, shoe-throwing giants, fairy bridges, witch-hunts, green butterflies – and a gold rush.

This landscape is accessible for walking, cycling, fishing, bird-watching and golf. Its archaeology, geology and mythology are interpreted through visitor trails and events organised by a good coastal Countryside Ranger service based at Inverness and a Forest Enterprise one at Lairg.

Try panning for gold in the Strath of Kildonan – there's still some left after the 1869 gold rush. Catch trout in Loch Shin or sit and watch the summer salmon leap Shin Falls. Explore the chequered history of Tain, or take a whisky tour round Glenmorangie Distillery. See the bird life of lovely Loch Fleet, a tidal basin with wonderful reflections in quiet weather, whose salt-marshes and mudlflats support migratory species like the Bar-tailed Godwit, especially in east winds, from April to May and August to October. The nectar of its unusual plants – the delicate pink Twinflower, Wintergreen, or Creeping Lady's Tresses – feeds rare butterflies like the Green Hairstreak and the Dark Green Fritillary.

Leaflets from Dornoch Tourist Information Centre detail self-guided walks; follow sign-posts along the disused railway track up the coast to Embo for great views of the Cairngorm Mountains, find a stone marked 1722 where the last Scottish witch was burned, see where the fairies built a bridge of sand across the Firth at Gizzen Briggs. Or simply go beach-combing along the sands.

For history buffs, a Pictish Trail leads from Nigg past Shandwick Bay to Tarbat and back along the Dornoch Firth to Edderton. There's an archaeological trail on Ord Hill and Ferrycroft Countryside Centre at Lairg.

The Black Isle is well-known for it beauty; fields full of crops, woods, pretty villages from which houses of pink sandstone or crisp white roughcast look out over the surrounding firths. Leave your troubles behind at the Cloutie Well – but make sure you don't pick up anyone else's by mistake. Wander the coastal path up to South Suter Viewpoint and see where two quarrelling giant cobblers chucked shoes at each other. Follow the cliffs round to the rockpools at Rosemarkie, or paddle along its pink sandy beach – complete with picnic facilities and loos. Contemplate

Cromarty Firth and Nigg from South Suter Viewpoint

Chanonry Point monument, near Fortrose, which marks the burning of the dreaded Brahan Seer. Cruise from Cromarty village to see the dolphins – and the oil rigs. And in August there's always Muir of Ord's Black Isle Agricultural Show.

The famous Victorian engineer Thomas Telford created the Caledonian Canal. Opened in 1922, its 42 locks lift ships to 33 metres above sea-level, a safer route than the Pentland Firth between the Atlantic and the North Sea for fishing boats, small cruisers, yachts and pleasure craft

INVERNESS & THE GREAT GLEN

Inverness is the capital of the Highlands. There's an airport and a train station, roads radiate to the farthest coasts carrying bus and post-bus services and the nerve centre of Highland Council Countryside Ranger Service is here. The River Ness passes picturesquely through the town, flowing eastwards from its famous loch around islands linked by pretty bridges and footpaths.

Loch Ness itself is part of the 100 mile-long Great Glen which splits Scotland, running south-west to Fort William, the result of an ancient tear-fault in the earth's crust, now a series of deep lochs and waterways forming the Caledonian Canal. Its broad towpaths are great for walking or cycling and you can hire boats or go fishing.

The accessibility of the Great Glen has been bringing people to Inverness since long before history. Legends abound, not only of Nessy the monster, but also of kings, saints, silver chains and an Irish princess.

Seabirds use the glen as a convenient flyway, so wildlife-watching can be rewarding. Ospreys, killed to extinction as 'vermin' by 1916, have made a comeback here. So have Red Kites, and you might see Redwings and Green Woodpeckers. Feral goats live near Loch Ness and there are deer, Pine Marten and Red Squirrel. No comment about monsters except to say the easiest way to be photographed beside a big plastic one is at Drumnadrochit Visitor Centre. Just take care not to be flattened by the tour buses.

After that, fancy a breath of fresh air? Try one of the Ranger service's self-guided walk maps around Loch Ness; one shows several routes through the countryside around Drumnadrochit. Up at the Divach Falls – once the site of an illicit whisky still – there are great views, or you can look for Dippers on the rivers down in Urquhart Woods by the loch.

Cycling along the Ness at Inverness

Rangers organise year-round events from Fort Augustus to Fort George; wander in General Wade's Footsteps imagining it's 1731 and you're one of his soldiers. Explore some of the 22 miles of footpaths around Foyers and Inverfarigaig, step back in time to Pictish days on Craig Phadraig, or go beach-combing at Dores. The route from North Kessock to Redcastle is level – go at low tide and look for the secret causeways built by early crannog-dwellers. Out on the Moray Firth near Fort George, Ardersier Common, once a rubbish tip, is a brilliant example of land-reclamation – find Food for Free like sweet wild raspberries among its 180 regenerated species of plants, flowers and trees, and identify the birds and frogs that have returned to feed there too, as you potter along its shore with the Rangers who cover the coast from Tain to Nairn.

Changing weather on a walk by the Moray Firth

Food for free walk – raspberries at Ardersier Common, once a rubbish tip, now reclaimed land

Cawdor Castle and garden

EAST **SCOTLAND**

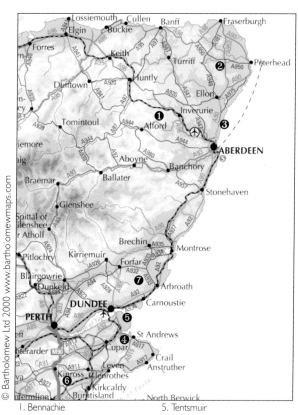

1. Bennachie
2. Aden Country Park
3. Balmedie Country Park
4. Craigtoun Country Park
5. Tentsmuir
6. Lochore Meadows
7. Crombie Country Park

© Bartholomew Ltd 2000 www.bartholomewmaps.com

INFORMATION

(OS Map Nos 27 – 30, 36 – 38, 43 – 45, 53, 54, 58, 59)

LOCAL AUTHORITIES

Aberdeenshire Council, Woodhill House, Westburn Road, Aberdeen AB16 5GB
Outdoor Services
Tel 01224 664534

Elgin Council Offices, High Street, Elgin IV30 1BX
Leisure Services Tel 01343 543451

Fife Council, Fife House, North Street, Glenrothes, Fife KY7 5LT
Tel 01592 416498

Angus Council, Market Street, Forfar, Angus DD8 3WA
Recreation Services
Tel 01307 461460

TOURIST INFORMATION CENTRES

ABERDEEN Tel 01224 632727

ALFORD (Seasonal)
Tel 01975 562052

DUNDEE Tel 01382 527527
www.angusanddundee.co.uk

ANSTRUTHER (Seasonal)
Tel 01333 311073

BALLATER (Seasonal)
Tel 01339 755306

BANFF (Seasonal)
Tel 01261 812419

BRAEMAR Tel 01339 741600

CRAIL (Seasonal)
Tel/fax 01333 450869

DUNFERMLINE (Seasonal)
Tel 01383 720999

ELGIN Tel 01343 542 666 or 01343 543388

FIFE Tel 01333 450869

FORTH BRIDGES
Tel 01383 417759

FRASERBURGH (Seasonal)
Tel 01346 518315

HUNTLY (Seasonal)
Tel 01466 792255

The characterful countryside of Moray, Aberdeenshire, Angus and Fife is designed on the grand scale. Huge rivers gush from the Grampian Mountains. Sculptural sweeps of farmland change with the seasons from rich brown plough to the green of growing corn, yellow rape, swathes of golden stubble dotted with bobbin-shaped straw bales, or pasture with Aberdeen Angus cattle scattered like liquorice sweeties.

The climate is generally drier and colder than in the

INVERURIE Tel 01467 620600
KINGDOM OF FIFE
Tel 01592 750 066
KIRKCALDY Tel 01592 267775
ST ANDREWS
Tel 01334 472021
STONEHAVEN (Seasonal)
Tel 01569 762806

COUNTRYSIDE RANGER SERVICES

Aberdeenshire District
Tel 01467 620981
Aboyne Ranger
Tel 01339 885262
Badenoch & Strathspey
Tel 01460 673551
Balmoral Estate Ranger Service
Tel 01338 55434
Benholm Ranger
Tel 01561 361969
Bennachie Ranger Centre
Tel 01467 681470
Buchan Countryside Group
Tel 01771 637394
Cawdor Estate
Tel 01667 404666
Glen Doll Tel 01575 550233
Glen Tanar Estate
Tel 01339 886451
Haddo Country Park
Tel 01651 851489
Haughton House Country Park
Tel 01336 2453/2107
Townhill Country Park
Tel 01383 725596
Inverurie Tel 01467 681470
Kincardine & Deeside District
Tel 01339 756144
Moray Estates
Tel 01309 672213
Rothiemurchus Estate
Tel 01479 810858
Silverburn, Fife Ranger Service
Tel 01333 429785
Spittal of Glen Muick
Tel 01339 755059

west. The moody North Sea can storm against the cliffs, or ripple sweetly along endless beaches, and sometimes sends an inflow of eerie haar that muffles the coast in mists for days on end. The castle that inspired the story of Dracula is here – and Royal Deeside.

Towns are mostly on the coast; Nairn, Banff, Aberdeen, Dundee and St Andrews, while the interior is full of interesting villages and historic towns like Ellon and Craigellachie, Oldmeldrum, Inverurie, Strichen, Ballater and Aboyne.

There's a lot going on. The summer months see a round of folk festivals and Highland Games, fiddlers' rallies, piping competitions and clan gatherings of various kinds. There are golf tournaments and events like the Aikey Fair and horse-market at historic Old Deer, and Fraserburgh's fish festival. Aberdeeen hosts an International Youth Festival, Keith has a folk festival and an agricultural show and Peterhead Harbour – one of the most important fishing ports of Europe – has an open day.

You can try the ancient sport of falconry near Huntly, rural art classes at Bennachie, hire a bike and travel miles of cycle tracks, or contact Aberdeenshire Council for details of their growing number of horse-riding trails. For history and atmosphere, choose a foggy day to trudge over ghostly Culloden Field near Inverness, scene of the last fateful Jacobite battle of 1746, or dare to visit the creepy ruins of Slains Castle, where Bram Stoker based the vampire's lair in his supernatural tale of Count Dracula. Nearby explore the Bullers o' Buchan, spectacular 200 feet deep chasms in the cliffs.

For a more extended experience of the landscape, walk the newly elongated Speyside Way from Buckie to Aviemore. If you prefer level coastlines, walk the 54 miles between Fraserburgh and Dyce on a route recently developed along a disused railway line.

Migrating sea-birds commute to and from their

breeding grounds along these coastlines. The Moray Firth is good for bird-watching, like the Waters of Philorth, the Loch of Strathbeg, Balmedie or St Cyrus. From the award-winning Visitor Centre at Montrose Basin you can refine your identification techniques through rows of binoculars. Further south, search for summer birds like Shovelers or Gadwalls on Forfar Loch, or winter migrants Pink-footed Geese and Goldeneyes.

If history is your thing, this is castle country. It's full of ancient piles dating from before the 12th century, some ruinous, some still lived-in, some fearsome, others pure fairytale. Fyvie Castle is famous for its grandeur, Corgarff for its successful restoration, Castle Fraser for its Z-plan architecture and its 'Laird's Lug' spyhole, Craigievar for its beauty.

If you're an off-road cycling enthusiast, head for Glenlivet Estate, famous for its cycle tracks, or have a go at bike-orienteering through Kirkhill Forest Trail Quest.

Go walking up the Deeside glens – Glen Doll is arguably the prettiest, well equipped with hostelries, camp sites and loos – up to the car park, and it's backed by famous mountains like Lochnagar.

This whole area is well-served by Countryside Rangers who work from their Local Authority centres or from the many Country Parks near the main towns. There's Aden near Peterhead, Balmedie and Haughton near Aberdeen, Camperdown and Clatto at Dundee, Monikie and Crombie by Carnoustie, Craigtoun outside St Andrews, Lochore Meadows and Townhill near Dunfermline, each offering a different set of experiences. Forest Enterprise runs Tentsmuir and there are famous old estates like those at Cawdor near Nairn, with its ancient oakwood, Crathes Castle, Haddo House and the Queen's estate at Balmoral, which welcome everyone. Rangers organise events in all of these, and work throughout the wider countryside. With their help you can have a first go at new skills or sports,

COUNTRY PARKS AND ESTATES

ADEN COUNTRY PARK, Hareshowe Farm and Waters of Philorth Tel 01771 622857

Aberdeenshire Farming Museum Tel 01771 622906

Book of Deer Project Tel 01771 613 666

BALMEDIE COUNTRY PARK Tel 01358 742396

BALMORAL ESTATE Tel 01339 742334

CAMPERDOWN COUNTRY PARK Tel 01382 432659 Wildlife Centre Tel 01382 432661

CAWDOR ESTATE (Seasonal) Tel 01667 404666

CLATTO COUNTRY PARK Tel 01382 889076

CRAIGTOUN COUNTRY PARK Tel 01333 429785 Eden Estuary Tel 01334 472151

CRATHES CASTLE Rangers' Office Tel 01330 844651

CROMBIE COUNTRY PARK Tel 01241 860360

GLENLIVET ESTATE Tel 01807 580283 Website www.crownestate.co.uk Glenlivet Distillery (seasonal) Tel 01542 783220

HADDO COUNTRY PARK Tel 01651 851489

HAUGHTON HOUSE COUNTRY PARK Tel 01975 562453

LOCHORE MEADOWS COUNTRY PARK Tel 01592 414300 Trout Fishery Tel 01592 414312 Riding Stables Tel 01592 861596 Windsurfing School Tel 01592 860264

MONIKIE COUNTRY PARK Tel 01382 370202 Angling Club (Seasonal) Tel 01382 370300

TOWNHILL COUNTRY PARK Tel 01383 725596

WALKS, LOCHS AND PLACES OF INTEREST

CULLODEN FIELD NTS Visitor Centre Tel 01463 790607

FORMARTINE AND BUCHAN WAY Tel 01771 637394

SPEYSIDE WAY Countryside Ranger, Boat o'Fiddich, Craigellachie Tel 01340 881266 Website www.moray.org/area/speyway/webpages/swhome.htm

GLEN DOLL Ranger service Tel 01575 550233

LOCH LEVEN NATURE RESERVE Tel 01577 864439

LOCH OF STRATHBEG RSPB Reserve Tel 01346 532017

MONTROSE BASIN Visitor Centre Tel 01674 676336

ST CYRUS Tel 01224 312266

USEFUL ORGANISATIONS

Glenrothes Ramblers' Association Tel 01592 757039

St Andrews Ramblers' Association Tel 01334 475396

Fife & Kinross Scottish Wildlife Trust Tel 01334 478946

All other Scottish Wildlife Trust info Tel 0131 312 7765

PUBLIC TRANSPORT

ABERDEEN AIRPORT Tel 01224 722331

SCOTRAIL Tel 0345 484950

BUSES

ABERDEEN Tel 01224 637047

FIFE Tel 01592 416060

DUNDEE Strathtay Scottish Tel 01382 228054

Footprints in the mud

photo: Andrew Morris

from simple rambling to making and flying your own kite.

Learn to 'read' the countryside on walks like 'Moss Identification for Beginners'. For children there are sessions on such topics as 'Who's for Dinner?', 'Rotten Walks' – about how Nature recycles, 'Beastie Bonanza' and 'Poisons and Prickles'. There's usually a small charge for these, but for some only a donation is invited.

Spotlit next are six sample places which show you the diversity of possibilities existing in this lovely part of Scotland.

A day out at Balmedie

ADEN COUNTRY PARK

The Waters of Philorth sound biblical but are in fact a collection of dunes, salt-marshes, mud banks and a reedy river course with a wealth of bird life

Aden is the most northerly Country Park in Scotland – and it's one of the best. Aden (pronounced 'Ahden') Rangers seem particularly talented at creative thinking. They run workshops on coracle building, arrange displays of Scottish music and dance, organise talks on topics like freshwater pearl mussels – and mastermind beach clean-ups or tree-planting sessions with volunteers. Visit the gannetry with them at Troup Head, learn how to use local plants for healing, how to appreciate raised bogs. Dogs do have to be kept under control for everyone's sake in the park, but these Rangers are dog-friendly, running special canine caper afternoons.

A good map in the car park helps orientate you. Nearby, the unusual semi-circular home farm buildings have been turned into an attractive complex of Visitor Centre, Farming Museum, coffee shop, loos and Ranger Centre. There's a large and well-equipped children's playground and, a short walk away, the roofless mansionhouse feels a little spooky till a bunch of cheery kids start chasing each other through the empty doors and windows of the grassy ground floor.

A one-mile circular walk will take you from the information base at the Visitor Centre, backwards through Aden's history to when it was part of St Drostan's Monastery of Deer, a Celtic church founded back in the 7th century. More recently it was a self-sufficient Victorian estate with its own gasworks, ice house, walled vegetable and fruit garden – and conservatory complete with banana trees.

Take a look at the award-winning video presentation in

Aden Visitor Centre and visitors

the Farming Museum, then walk the 800 yards through the woods to 'Hareshowe', a cleaned-up working farm frozen in time between the 1930s and 50s. This was the period when tractors began to replace horses. It's still run according to the crop rotation practised then, with seasonal demonstrations and cost-free guided tours every half hour.

Aden is now owned and managed by Aberdeenshire Council for the enjoyment of both locals and visitors. There are clear leaflets showing you where to go on wildlife walks, tree trails or 'Doric danders'. Walk some of the adjoining Formartine and Buchan Way. Aden Country Park offers a satisfyingly complete set of rural experiences.

If you're in luck, you can drop in on one of the Farming Museum's old style cookery demonstrations and munch on delicate hot-buttered hand-made oatcakes, or steaming floury girdle-scones.

photo: Andrew Morris

Fishing on the Spey

THE SPEYSIDE WAY & GLENLIVET ESTATE

Walk the Speyside Way and see Scotland at its grandest. Linking the Moray Firth to Aviemore, with spurs to Dufftown and Tomintoul, it's a way-marked long-distance walking route totalling 84 miles. Travelling inland from the sea at Buckie, head south towards the sun via Loch Garten to Aviemore. Or turn left at Ballindalloch and climb 15 miles through visitor-friendly whisky distilleries, up to Cairn Daimh (Hill of the Stags) 1,850 ft above sea-level, to Tomintoul, Moray's highest village. While up there, explore Glenlivet Estate.

Although the Way is mainly intended for walkers, you're welcome to ride your horses on the 17 miles from Dufftown to Ballindalloch – provided they'll cope with two fords and a few single-rail stiles. You can cycle the same stretch, and between Nethy Bridge and Aviemore. Most people walking the whole Way leave their dogs at home, but there are short sections where a well-trained dog can run free. Notices show clearly where and when dogs aren't allowed, often because of sheep farming.

Spring snow on the Speyside Way at Craigellachie

The Way makes a good introduction to long distance walking, much of it following footpaths, 16th century drove roads and disused railways, suitable for families and the less fit. The Tomintoul spur is steeper and in some places without actual

photo: Alison Wilson

Watching for fish

constructed paths. Depending on your level of fitness and preferred speed, you can cover the whole Way in 5 days but why hurry? You'll have far more fun if you give it a week or more, passing through lively villages and tranquil habitats varying from moorland to river valley and seashore.

The Countryside Ranger Service is on the Way, at Craigellachie, in Boat o' Fiddich Cottage. Most weekdays from June to September you can call in for up-to-date information, useful safety advice, maps, and leaflets on accommodation, shops, pubs, doctors, banks, eating places and more.

What might you see? The old railway sections have masses of wildflowers and butterflies in summer. The ever-shifting shingles of Spey Bay are home to sea-birds like Shelduck and Terns. Historically, there's Tugnet fishing station and an ice-house once used for salmon, there's Garmouth Viaduct, and Ballindalloch railway bridge over the Spey.

Glenlivet's new visitor centre up at Tomintoul has an Estate Ranger to help you get the best out of the 90 square miles of rolling hills around the straths of the rivers Avon and Livet. This magnificent estate welcomes walkers, mountain bikers, fishers, birdwatchers and skiers – and folk who just want to enjoy a dauner in unrivalled peace. Sheltered by the Cairngorms from the worst of the winds, it's remarkably dry. You can enjoy walking, cycling or horse-riding over a network of 60 miles of way-marked paths leading you into remote areas. Winter snow here tends to last into Spring and you can ski downhill on the Lecht, cross-country over the hills or along forest tracks. Fantastic.

Watch for a wide variety of upland birds – Crossbills, Siskins and Redpolls – and juniper scrub supports Black Grouse. High above you, Kestrels and Hen Harriers soar,

Glenlivet cyclist
Speyside Way at Ballindalloch

and in the trees you might even see a Red Squirrel. Signs of human habitation go back a long way, like Knock Earth House, Packhorse Bridge and Drumin Castle, once the 14th century fortress of the Wolf of Badenoch.

If you're cycling on Glenlivet Estate, leave your dog at home. Certain routes are closed to visitors in the stalking season (around April–August and again in October) and it's healthy to check with the Ranger where the guns are during the grouse-shooting season (mid-August to late October).

Crathes roses

CRATHES CASTLE

Of all Royal Deeside's castles, Crathes is one of the best, with something to offer most people. This fairytale, turreted, 16th century tower-house has grounds with miles of way-marked trails for walking, jogging, pottering and orienteering, including one designed for wheelchair users. There's also a particularly good Countryside Ranger Service.

Crathes Estate is 600 acres of woods and farmland, including almost 4 acres of award-winning garden. Take your wheelchair for a run along one of their two trails. There's a children's playground and a visitor centre with exhibitions interpreting the varied history of Crathes and its Lairds.

Grampian Rangers organise an excellent programme of guided walks here and around the district. Events include such outings as an Easter Treasure Trail, a 4 a.m. listen-in to Crathes dawn chorus, an afternoon children's Beastie Bonanza, a bird-watch at Fyvie Castle, an evening wildlife watch at Drum Castle and a session at Crathes on the estate's history. Others take place at Castle Fraser, Pitmedden Garden and Leith Hall.

For some of these there's a charge, some ask for a donation only. Rangers do environmental visits to interested groups, run a lively Young Naturalists Club for 7 – 11s and an interesting Green Action Group for 11 – 16s. At 16 you can become a Conservation Volunteer.

What might you see, wandering through the estate? Find out what a ha-ha looks like – and why it's there. Spot an otter up the Coy Burn – but they're shy. Rabbits breed in profusion and are a laugh a minute. Give yourself a headache

Crathes garden and visitors

watching Green Woodpeckers knock holes in tree-trunks. Give yourself a fright at dusk, encountering Daubenton's Bats. Damp-loving trees and plants that have vanished from drained farmland still thrive here – look for Alder, Brooklime or White-flowered Watercress. Search for the 19th century Arboretum and trees wrapped in wreaths of sweetly perfumed honeysuckle. Watch trout in the Millpond. See how Nature has re-covered a quarry in wild flowers like pink Campion, green Alkanet and blue Forget-me-not, with all the butterflies that feed on them. Yew trees sprout from the granite crags of the geologically interesting Crathes Mass and in Spring, toads, frogs and newts hop around the damp cliff at 'Caroline's Garden'.

Crathes Castle and gardens has miles of way-marked trails for walking, jogging, pottering and orienteering, including one designed for wheelchair users

Obedient dogs are welcome to run about off their leashes on the trails. Drinking-water is thoughtfully provided for them plus a shady car-park so they don't overheat while you explore the people-only areas.

Craigton Country Park – lots for children to do

CRAIGTOUN COUNTRY PARK & NORTH-EAST FIFE

Craigtoun Country Park sits on a hillside two miles from St Andrews. Its 50 acre site is really a beautiful garden with play places. It's hugely popular. Groomed lawns surround a loch complete with a fantasy Dutch village. Hire a rowing boat in summer, admire flowerbeds bursting with colour, or chug round on the miniature steam-train. There's putting, crazy golf, bowls, and children can head for the large play-park, trampolines, a bouncy castle or the adventure playground, well away from the peace of the Rose Garden, the Italian Garden or the Walled Garden and glasshouses. Talk to exotic trees like Sequoia, Cedar and Cypress or commune with the aviary birds. Visit pet's corner. There are picnic spaces aplenty and strategically place loos. Sometimes bands play in the open air theatre and there's a cafeteria.

Two events happen here each summer; Craigtoun Fair and a Vintage Rally. Countryside Rangers lead guided walks here and outwith the park. One of these will take you wandering the rights of way from St Andrews, visiting the Lade Braes, Lumbo Den and Craigtoun Den.

Fife Countryside Rangers specialise in watery environments. They're very much concerned with the development of wildlife and the regeneration of sites such as old quarries like Burnie Loch. There's also Cameron Reservoir, the new Forth-Tay Coastal Path, the internationally

At Tentsmuir you walk through thyme-scented dunes and see a beach that seems to stretch to the horizon, at low tide. Almost flat, when the sea does appear on a wind-free day, it's shallow enough for toddlers and paddlers

important Eden Estuary Nature Reserve, and Tentsmuir, a vast expanse of woodland and beach.

Young people make themselves useful, locally – St Monance Youth Group help maintain the Coastal Path and Leuchars Nature Trail, while receiving training – and Rangers welcome any practical projects from groups of teenagers who have their own leader.

To reach Tentsmuir you need wheels for the long road in, through deep deciduous woodland then coniferous forest, interspersed with secret fields full of horses. You park romantically beneath tall coastal pines. And you have to pay, in spite of there being no facilities.

Beachcombers might find sponges, Mermaid's Purses, Razor shells and predatory Necklace shells. Birdwatchers might see Velvet Scoters, Red-breasted Mergansers and Bar-tailed Godwits, while animal life includes Foxes, Roe Deer and Common Seals. In the dunes, search for wildflowers like Glasswort, Sea Aster and Restharrow.

The Eden Estuary has very dangerous tides. Sensible advice is – wear wellies and stay above the tide-line. Sandbars look tempting – but as the sea rises you can be cut off, and the softening mud gives you that sinking feeling too late to be useful. Two areas are shown on the map as sanctuaries – strictly for the birds. But anyone can look, so for a fascinating insight into bird life take a pair of binoculars or a telescope.

Canoe class at Lochore
Meadows, land reclaimed
from coal mining

LOCHORE MEADOWS

Lochore Meadows is a thoroughly modern example of what a Country Park can be. But it wasn't always like this. The story of how these 1,200 acres were turned from the ugliest of brownfield sites into the present idyll of rolling grassland, loch and woods for the enjoyment of everyone, is a slice of Scottish history. Explore the farthest limits of the park and discover an ancient castle, avoid falling into Petrie's Ponds, look for Lady's Smocks – and meet the Great Mary.

There is so much you can do here. Relax on the beach, follow the many trails, coorie in the bird hide, slither down the slide in the adventure playground, take your wheelchair on tour, go fishing, and watch the wildlife. The Countryside Rangers' base is in the well-appointed Visitor Centre, plus a good cafeteria and loos, and one of six car parks is conveniently close. Picnic near the beach or cook up dinner on one of the bookable barbecues.

Wheelchair-users are welcome here. Exercise on smooth level paths for miles, watch birds from a hide, or mess about in the 'wheely-boat'. Within the park there's a separately-run riding stable. Kids can 'Own a Pony for a Day', 'Young Trojans' is a club for pony-mad 7+ children and Party Treks are for birthdays. Golfers enjoy the course here, and fishing enthusiasts catch trout from banks or boats. For dog-owners there's a doggy leaflet listing the best places to enjoy the park – and what to do if your dog 'has an accident' in the wrong place!

Lochore windsurfing school

Try canoeing, power boating, hillwalking or orienteering with instructors at Loch Ore Outdoor Pursuits Centre, where equipment is available for people with disabilities. Meadies Midges and Young Gnaturalists are two junior nature clubs. Once grown-up, you're welcome to join Fife Conservation Volunteers.

History enthusiasts can seek for evidence of the park's murky past. Hut circles show human habitation began around 2,000 BC. Centuries of working the land led to 1160, when David de Lochore built a stronghold to defend it . Six centuries later Captain Parks (!) bought the estate and promptly drained the loch to create more agricultural land. But the ground remained soggy. The coal industry appeared and by the end of the 19th century mining was in full flow. This became the major activity and the area was covered with industrial buildings and waste. Then suddenly, between 1963 and '67 all the pits were closed. Mass unemployment followed and the site became a refuse tip. Pit props were removed and the ground subsided.

But gradually, Loch Ore returned, to fill the hole. Fife County Council decided to reclaim this land for the people. At times it must have seemed an impossible task, but 9 years and £1million later, Lochore Meadows as we see it today, was created. The winding tower Great Mary remains, a piece of industrial archaeology.

Rangers monitor the increasing numbers of birds using the loch. Look out for Sedge Warblers, Wigeon and Kestrels. Wildflowers now flourish – can you find Field Woodrush, Comfrey or Lady's Smock?

Camperdown is designed on the grand scale. An imposing gateway and a long drive takes you up to a huge mansionhouse – lawns and a golf-course are laid out

DUNDEE & ANGUS COUNTRY PARKS

The Dundee area is well-served with local authority Country Parks. Crombie and Monikie are so close you can walk from one to the other. Camperdown and Clatto are separated only by woodland.

From Camperdown the view includes mature trees – and the high-rise flats of Dundee. Go down the hill and discover all sorts of goodies for the family, like a zoo, a boating pond, a big children's playground, loos, a mini racing-car circuit and Dundee City Council's Ranger service.

Clatto is a water-facility, enclosed in woodland, where people can learn about boating of all sorts. It's much used by school and college groups for this, and there are interesting birds about. Clatto Country Park is linked to Camperdown through spooky Templeton woods which might be okay during daylight with your German Shepherd escort, but which you might prefer to stay out of after dark.

Crombie Country Park has a reservoir at its heart, complete with island. Once an estate, its Main Lodge now houses a good Visitor Centre. Angus Council's Countryside Ranger service operates here, though not continuously. Rangers organise guided walks all over the county and help with fieldwork activities for schools and clubs. They run a cheery Young Naturalists' Club – try their Unnatural Walk. Annual events include family days like the Mini Highland Games, workshops on practical crafts like drystane dyking

A Monikie windsurfer has landed!

and school holiday specials for children. There's a 36-point orienteering course, plus maps and clipboards – but you have to bring your own pencil. Try Practical Conservation. People with special needs are welcome here and may park at Main Lodge. Loos and a lochside hide are all easily reached.

On your own, try the Discovery Trail and find who the Beaker People were and how they lived, seek out Hairy Nicoll's Cottage, see where stone kists were found, or go roaming in Fallaws Wood or Wedderswell Wood. You can also fish from a boat here and there are barbecue and picnic facilities. In summer there's a public marquee in case shelter is needed. There is a fairly long walk in from the car park, but this means Crombie is very peaceful

Because there's a lot of animal wildlife, only guide dogs are allowed at Crombie. Grebes, Coot, Duck and Moorhens nest around the loch, and long skeins of Pink-foot and Greylag geese sweep down from the sky on their winter migrations. In the woods, listen and look for Crossbills, Green Woodpeckers and Tree Creepers.

Both Crombie and Monikie Rangers host Adult Learners' Weeks to which you're invited to bring your memorabilia and enjoy a picnic. In June there's a Wildlife Week. Up at Monikie, bird-life and boats are the thing and the Countryside Rangers run a great collection of events. Try bodging, balsam-bashing or bat-box building. Have a go at wildlife gardening, windsurfing, dinghy sailing or canoeing. There's a summer Water Fun Day for children who can swim, and a Canoe Club.

West Highland Way at Glen Coe

HEART of **SCOTLAND**

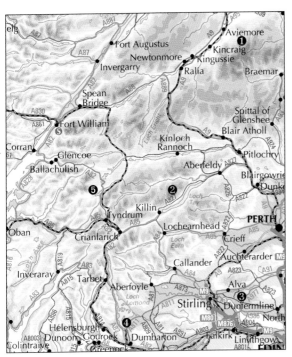

1. Glenmore Forest Park
2. Ben Lawers
3. Gartmore Dam Country Park
4. Balloch Castle
5. Glencoe and Bridge of Orchy

© Bartholomew Ltd 2000 www.bartholomewmaps.com

INFORMATION

OS Map Nos 26, 27, 34, 35, 36, 41, 42, 43, 50, 51, 52, 57, 58, 64, 65

LOCAL AUTHORITIES

Clackmannanshire Council , Greenfield, Alloa, FK10 2AD
Tel 01259 450000

Falkirk Council, Municipal Buildings, Falkirk, FK1 5RS
Tel 01259 450000

Fife Council, Fife House, North Street, Glenrothes, FIFE KY7 5LT
Tel 01592 414141

Perth and Kinross Council, PO Box 77, 1 High Street, Perth PH1 5PH
Tel 01738 475000

Stirling Council, Viewforth, Stirling, FK8 2ET
Tel 01786 443322

TOURIST INFORMATION CENTRES

AVIEMORE Tel 01479 810363

DUMBARTON/LOCH LOMOND
Tel 01389 753533

FALKIRK Tel 01324 620244

GLASGOW Tel 0141 204 4400

PERTH TIC Tel 01738 450600

STIRLING Tel 01786 475019

USEFUL ORGANISATIONS

SCOTTISH NATURAL HERITAGE (East Highland Area) Achantoul Aviemore PH22 1QD
Tel 01479 810477

Glasgow – Loch Lomond CYCLEWAY Tel 0141 572 0234

SUSTRANS Infoline
Tel 0117 9290888

CAIRNGORMS
The Cairngorm Reindeer Herd
Tel 01479 861228

Cairngorm Chairlift Company
Tel 01479 861261

etween the Great Glen and the Central belt, the heart of Scotland has landscapes and lochs on a large scale. The massive Cairngorms lower themselves to moorlands spreading from Kingussie to Loch Rannoch. Southward, the mountains separate and lochs grow bigger till the tear-drop shape of Loch Lomond splits Argyll from Stirlingshire. Across its south end, the Highland Boundary Fault begins the Lowlands. Linking the whole area north to south is the famous West Highland Way and drawing a line from coast

CENTRES OF INTEREST

ROTHIEMURCHUS ESTATE
Visitor Centre
Tel 01479 812345
Rothiemurchus Shooting
Ground Tel 01479 811272

GLENMORE FOREST PARK
Tel 01479 861221
Loch Morlich Watersports
Centre Tel 01479 861221

Highland Folk Museum,
Newtonmore
Tel 01738 475000

PERTH AND KINROSS
COUNCIL Countryside Ranger
Service Tel 01738 475000

BLAIR CASTLE
Tel 01796 481207
Pony Trekking
Tel 01796 481263

ATHOLL ESTATES Ranger
Service Tel 01796 481646 (am)
Tel 01796 481355 (pm)

FORESTRY COMMISSION
Tel 01350 723255

KILLIECRANKIE NTS Ranger
Service Tel 01350 728641

TAY FOREST PARK
Queens View Visitor Centre
Tel 01350 727284
Tay Forest Walks Tel 01350
723255

LOCH OF THE LOWES
WILDLIFE CENTRE
Tel 01350 727337

BEN LAWERS Mountain Visitor
Centre Tel 01567 820397

STIRLING COUNCIL
RANGER SERVICE
Tel 01786 442875

QUEEN ELIZABETH FOREST
PARK Tel 01877 382258

PLEAN COUNTRY PARK
Tel 01786 442541

CLACKMANNANSHIRE
COUNCIL Ranger Service
Tel 01259 452000

GARMORN DAM COUNTRY
PARK Tel 01259 214319

LOCH LOMOND NATIONAL
PARK HQ in Balloch
Tel 01389 753311

to coast, the Forth and Clyde Canal is the scene of Scotland's biggest Millennium project.

This central heartland is arguably Scotland's greatest play area. While much of it is also farmed and there are small pockets of industry, here you can try every outdoor pastime, from the most extreme sports to the quietest and most contemplative arts.

The Cairngorm Mountains form Britain's highest land mass. The great ice-age glaciers flowing down from them created the river valleys of the north east. Later, the way of life here produced a tough warrior breed strong enough to repel Roman invaders. Now the area around Aviemore is best known for winter sports and birds of prey. Further south, Ben Lawers and the mountains of Glencoe are also popular with skiers, climbers, hillwalkers and birdwatchers.

The rolling landscapes of Perth and Kinross look less fierce. Reaching south from the Grampians, sheltered by the higher Cairngorms from the worst of the north wind, they're full of attractive towns, pretty villages, lovely glens and great sweeps of farmland topped with heathery moors.

Stirlingshire, often regarded as the gateway to the Highlands, has the grand Ochil Hills and the Trossachs, part of Loch Lomond National Park, is popular with Sunday walkers from Glasgow. Tiny Clackmannanshire has big ideas for outdoor activities.

The Central Belt stretches through East Dunbartonshire, North Lanarkshire, Falkirk and West Lothian linking the River Clyde with the Forth through some of Scotland's most industrial areas. But even here, there's lots to do out of doors.

THE CAIRNGORMS

The Cairngorm mountains are famous for their size, dangerous climate, winter sports and tough climbs. Every winter we see TV pictures of snow-covered men and dogs struggling through blizzards yet again to rescue a benighted adventurer – it's true, these mountains are to be respected. Rising to 4,296 ft, they can present literally Arctic conditions in Winter. But there's more to the Cairngorms than winter mountain climbing.

It's a great part of Scotland to visit in Spring, summer and autumn, there are flat lochs and rolling woodlands – and you don't have to risk your life to have a good time.

There are good mountain-biking routes, hundreds of miles of mountain paths, forest trails and lochside tracks to wander, a wealth of wildlife to watch, quiet lochs to fish, boat on, photograph or paint, and great Countryside Rangers around, to guide you.

On a good summer's day it's worth taking the chairlift up Cairn Gorm and with the snow off the tops you get a good feel of the battered granite mountains. You just might see a Ptarmigan, or maybe a Golden Eagle far out in the sky, and if you see a Reindeer, don't worry, you're not turning into Santa Claus; Scotland's only herd roam about. Anywhere between here and Loch Garten you might see Osprey flying around.

It's fine to walk on these mountains if you're sensible; listen to weather reports, good local advice, take all-weather gear, maps and compass – and stick to paths. It's also true there's no shelter up there from wind or rain, let alone

BALLOCH CASTLE COUNTRY PARK
Tel 01389 758216

COUNTRYSIDE RANGER SERVICE
The Park Centre, Luss
Tel 01436 860601

The Park Centre, Balmaha
Tel 01360 870470
Ben Lomond Tel 01360 870224

WEST HIGHLAND WAY
GLEN NEVIS Visitor Centre
Tel 01397 705922

GLENCOE NTS
Visitor Centre Tel 01855 811296

Ranger Service
Tel 01389 758216

Ranger Service
Fort William – Tyndrum
Tel 01397 705922

FORTH, CLYDE AND UNION CANALS
Canal Ranger West
Tel 0141 332 9115
Canal Ranger East
Tel 01506 857725

PUBLIC TRANSPORT

INVERNESS AIRPORT
Tel 01463 232471

British Airways Tel 0345 222111

Easyjet Tel 0870 6000000

SCOTRAIL enquiries
Tel 0845 748 4950

BUSES

Highland Country Buses Tel 01479 811566

Citylink Tel 08705 505050
National Express Tel 0990 808080

Cairngorm rest – starting at the top car park at Cairn Gorm, from where the chairlift machinery whisks people to the summit restaurant, you'll often find an experienced Ranger on duty

Watersports on Loch Morlich with the Cairngorms behind

The Highland Folk Museum at Newtonmore has its own Countryside Ranger service

blizzards. But on a good day the views are stupendous, and in the shady summer corries you might discover a rare alpine plant, like Arctic Mouse-ear.

Nearer Aviemore, Rothiemurchus Estate Countryside Rangers have a great programme of guided walks and events. With them, discover the estate's social history, and what's running, flying or swimming about on the wildlife scene. Try a tour by tractor and trailer or a Landrover Safari, try orienteering, or its gentler relative, pathfinding. Go fishing – there's a specially created trout stream and lochs – and you can buy permits or hire equipment. Sometimes there are salmon in the Spey.

At Rothiemurchus there's Caledonian pineforest, Highland Cattle, deer, a Visitor Centre, good shops, a restaurant and loos. It's worth taking the time to wander the quiet footpaths around Loch an Eilean, too. The island castle there was once the stronghold of the fearsome 'Wolf of Badenoch', Alexander Stewart.

Walkers setting off from Perth

PERTHSHIRE

Perthshire, one of Scotland's prettiest counties, offers you a wealth of estates, forests, lochs, rivers, mountains, history and archaeology to discover. There are Pictish stones, the one-time seat of Scottish royalty to explore and lots to do, especially in summer.

Scone Palace has its Game Conservancy Fair, Dunkeld has an Arts Festival, Perth hosts a regatta, Pitlochry does its famous summer theatre season, Kenmore's fascinating Crannog Centre might be celebrating Midsummer with a Celtic Food Festival, Newburgh races Cobble boats, there are Gala Weeks, Highland Games, shearing contests and music events all over the area.

Countryside Rangers run guided walks, some for children; send them skiddling on a wet welly walk up river Garry, taking the air in a flying wildlife workshop, or crawling around bug hunting at Killiecrankie.

Picnickers on Kinnoul Hill

Other things to do? Try Lady Mary's Walk – bat-hunting around Crieff – for a thrilling night out, or ghost-busting at Blair Castle. More peacefully, stroll along the banks of the silvery Sunday Tay.

Peacocks strut the parklands of Blair Castle Estate. You can wander miles of Nature Trails,

Everyone can see what the soldier saw at Killiecrankie, where there's a good Visitor Centre and loos near the car park – and some very steep walking

picnic, or try the self-service restaurant. There's a Countryside Ranger service, a play area for children, a shop and loos.

Try the Queen's View at Tay Forest Park's Visitor Centre. Leave your dog at home and book yourself on to a guided walk with the Forest Rangers. Meet old granny pines in the Black Wood of Rannoch, identify trees in all seasons at Faskally, discover legends associated with Weem Woodland trees, animals and plants, try the Twilight Zone, searching for creatures of the night around Craigvinean. Your dog is welcome in the forest except on guided walks. Cyclists too.

Ben Lawers Visitor Centre has altitude; 12,000 acres of hillside, a car park and loos. There's a Young Naturalists' Club and, in July and August, the Countryside Rangers do special Tuesday walks for children. More strenuous walk topics include Mountain Flowers and Managing a Mountain. Ben Lawers' limestone base encourages plants like Roseroot, Angelica, Oak Fern and Wood Anemone. You might see Mountain Hares high up, and possibly Peregrines.

Dunkeld Village Countryside Ranger Centre

There's also a Countryside Ranger service based above the Tourist Information Centre at Dunkeld Cross. Their leaflets detail a great network of paths to explore. Stretch your legs on a strenuous 4 mile walk up Birnam Hill and you might see Blackcock feeding on blaeberries. At the Hermitage some of the drystane dykes are over 200 years old. Look over the old bridge, built by the 3rd Duke of Atholl in 1774. You might see a salmon or two waiting to leap the waterfalls tumbling below his folly, Ossian's Hall. Look out for shy Red Squirrels on the way to Ossian's Cave – no-one knows when this hermit's cell was constructed.

Wander easy paths through lofty woods around Dunkeld's Hermitage, in the footsteps of Wordsworth, Mendelssohn, Turner and Beatrix Potter

Visit Loch of the Lowes to look for Ospreys, Otters or Great-crested Grebes from the observation hides, one of which is suitable for wheelchairs. High-powered binoculars and telescopes are available and CCTV brings marvellous views of wildlife right into the Centre. Rangers and volunteer staff help answer your questions. Er – what exactly is the Haggis Stone?

STIRLINGSHIRE & THE CENTRE

Stirlingshire and neighbouring Clackmannanshire each has its own distinctive character and diversity.

Tiny Clackmannanshire, sheltered beneath the Ochil Hills, has excellent walking and biking along its Countryside Network. Local horse riders have helped the council create a new trail. All pass through lovely Gartmorn Dam Country Park, 370 acres of open countryside and woodland. Fish the reservoir, observe local and migrating birds from hides. Once the Earl of Mar's seat, Gartmorn became industrial, then fell derelict till Nature reclaimed it and is now beloved of riders, walkers, wheelchair users, dog-owners, buggy-pushers and cyclists.

Clackmannanshire Countryside Rangers, based in Alloa, organise a wonderful variety of events here and throughout the 'wee county'. Turn up for a Wildflower Wander, find out what heals – and what has Sinister Connections. Take a 5 mile hike along the Gartmorn Ridge. Find inspiration with Art in the Park. Encounter fascinating flying mammals on Bat watching sessions, sample the geology of the majestic Ochils, or go orienteering. Try fishing from the bank or a boat; there's often an instructor on hand, there's a junior angling summer-school and occasional fishing contests for everyone. 'Gartmorn Cygnets', the monthly junior nature club, have sessions on scary animal sculptures, Snowy Survival or being Inspector Detectors, tracking down wildlife. Gartmorn has a useful Visitor Centre right beside the car-park, and loos – open all week in summer, otherwise weekend afternoons only. Level,

smooth paths lead wheelchair drivers along the lochside to a sunken garden. There are picnic places and two bookable barbecue sites.

Stirling Council Countryside Rangers take guided walks anywhere in the county. Cycle Loch Katrine, join in the Doune and Dunblane Fling, wander the Wet Wilderness at Fallin, or seek the Wizard of Abbey Craig. Learn about upland management on Ben Venue, walk the spout of Ballochleam or enjoy the loveliness of Allan Water.

And look, behind the village of Plean, for an old estate, once complete with mansion house, walled garden, policies and a wealth of coal mines. Plean Country Park is a largely undiscovered treasure, with three waymarked trails. Walk its two disused bings and see a prime example of pioneer plant colonisation. Birch trees seeded themselves first; Oak and Rowan, Scots pine and Hawthorn followed. Birds, wildflowers and insects complete the resurgence of wildlife. Local people, many of whose fathers once mined here, now happily walk their dogs, their children and their grannies through the greenery while schools come to study industrial history.

Count the fluorescent Damselflies darting round the

High quality, waymarked paths link Dollar, Menstrie, Alloa, Dunfermline, Clackmannan and Tillicoultry, while interpretation boards explain their interesting industrial history

Butterfly orchid in Plean meadow

pond and watch its watery wildlife. In front of the burned-out mansion the Great Meadow, left to its own devices for decades, is one of the few true wildflower meadows you'll see in Scotland. In summer, awash with colour from Harebells, Campion, Spotted and Butterfly Orchids, daisies and buttercups, it's buzzing with the bees and butterflies that feed on them.

Countryside Ranger events here might include an Easter Egg Hunt, a Festival of Natural Crafts with a wildfood cook-up and a chance to try dyeing, or a late summer look at nature's recyclers – funghi.

There's a horse-riding trail and improving access for disabled people. Open to the public during daylight hours, Plean has good car parking, but few facilities apart from loos. Unattended most of the time, it suffers the occasional consequences.

Surrounded by big mountains, forests, rivers and lochs, Loch Lomond offers dreamily peaceful places, scope for all kinds of interests and leaves plenty of space for action

LOCH LOMOND NATIONAL PARK

Larking about in Loch Lomond at the village of Luss

Loch Lomond and its surrounding landscape is hugely popular. Tourists flock here all summer long, and generations of people from Glasgow and the Central Belt have enjoyed its year-round freedoms. Our first National Park extends to include everywhere from Balloch to beyond Lochearnhead, from the 'Arrochar Alps' to the Trossachs.

Cyclists are welcome on Forestry Commission tracks throughout the park, walkers are spoilt for choice, with access to open hillsides, glens, riversides and the West Highland Way. If you ride a wheelchair or push a buggy, try the old road up the west side of Loch Lomond, starting from Firkin Point with its car park and loos. Head for viewpoints like Rubha Mor or Rubha Dubh to do that painting, watch the wildlife or count the boats.

Wildlife you might creep up on in the quieter parts of the area include Deer, Otter, Mink, Golden Eagle, Ptarmigan and Blue Hare. In winter you might see Whooper Swans and lots of migrating ducks and geese. 200 species of birds have been recorded here.

Loch Lomond itself began with the melting of ice-age glaciers. Conic Hill and a string of islands are part of the Highland Boundary Fault, where the rugged northern mountains end and the fertile fields of the Lowlands begin. 5,000 years ago the earliest people paddled their canoes along these shores in search of 18 species of fish, including the unique Powan, which still exists – just. The first missionary was St Kessog, an Irish monk who set up a

The ground floor of Balloch Castle makes a spacious Visitor Centre complete with displays, attractive murals, shop, loos and tearoom

monastery on the island of Inchtavannach and was martyred near Luss in 520 AD. Luss is a sweetie-box-pretty conservation village, alias Glendarroch, scene of popular Scottish soap-opera *High Road*. Islands nearby include Inchlonaig, where Bruce grew yew trees to provide springy wood for his bowmen. On Inchconnachan, Luss villagers once distilled illicit whisky.

You can explore Loch Lomond and its islands by boat from Luss, Balmaha, Tarbet, Inveruglas, Ardlui and Balloch. The ruined 13th century Balloch Castle, ancient seat of the Earls of Lennox, was recycled into the present castellated gothic version in 1808 and visited by Sir Walter Scott. Explore 200 acres of Victorian landscape, wander the drovers' route through Moat Wood along the lochside, stop and relax on one of its shingly coves, walk through woodland and discover the walled garden. Picnic down on the shore and watch the bustling boat life of Balloch. Or tiptoe down Fairy Glen, where once the wee folk danced in the moonlight by the Burn of Balloch.

Balloch trunk

More visible than fairies, Countryside Rangers, many with special qualifications in water safety, work from Balloch Castle and will be happy to show you the present-day magic of the whole area, on a variety of guided walks.

Out on the hills, dogs are welcome on leads. On the water, the weather can change surprisingly quickly, the wind funnelling between the hills in strange ways, so it's best to ask advice about where – and whether – to venture out.

The Trossachs sweep away to the north and east behind Ben Lomond. Queen Elizabeth Park near Aberfoyle is well worth a visit. Wonderful views alternate with sheltered riverside paths for good walking. The visitor centre is useful, but both it and all its facilities are closed even on sunny weekends in winter. Seems daft.

THE WEST HIGHLAND WAY

The West Highland Way is 95 miles of Long Distance Footpath, stretching between Scotland's highest mountain and its biggest city, passing its most fearsome glen and its most famous loch. Well provided with interesting stopping-off places, it leads you along 18th century military roads built to control the Jacobite clans, 19th century drove roads and disued 20th century railways. There's also a good Countryside Ranger Service operating from centres at Balloch and Glen Nevis.

From Glasgow, the route passes over the lowlands, around the eastern, least populated shore of Loch Lomond, crosses the Highland Boundary Fault and takes you upland into Glencoe and through the Highlands to the very foot of Ben Nevis.

If you want to walk the whole Way, the first bit of advice is not to carry too much. Reasonably fit, you might do it in ten days. Some walkers will average 13 miles a day. But it's much more enjoyable to take your time, allow for an extra day here and there in particularly lovely spots, especially cheery watering-holes – or simply to stand and stare at the wildlife and beauty around you without trying to break

Blackrock Cottage, West Highland Way

Rest your feet and see the view from Glencoe chairlift

any records. You might prefer to do it a bit at a time over several weekends, and this is easily organised because access is feasible at the crossing-points of roads or in communities. Because section-walking is so popular, favourite parts of the path can be crowded – which also means more worn, eroded and rough than others, particularly at the south end. Stay in a variety of hostelries en route, like Inverarnan at the head of Loch Lomond, Inveroran near Bridge of Orchy, or Kingshouse in Glencoe , or camp carefully.

The West Highland Way is for walkers. The path is not really suitable for cycling or horse-riders. Dogs aren't encouraged either – and are actually forbidden on Conic Hill, Inversnaid to Crianlarich and Tyndrum to Bridge of Orchy. Be careful in May, though, when you're liable to be mown down by motorbikes during the Scottish Motorcycle

Trials between Bridge of Orchy and Fort William. Check with the Rangers at that time.

The Way varies in difficulty from south to north. At the southern end there are sections suitable for less-experienced walkers or family groups, but north of Rowardennan the path becomes more demanding and increasingly remote, there's little shelter, and the track's rough and muddy. So if you're new to the route, start in the south. You'll have a gentler warm-up than in the northern section. Good strong purpose-built, comfortable walking boots and reliable wet weather, windproof clothing are essential. Take maps and a compass and carry food.

The West Highland Way must be Scotland's most cosmopolitan footpath – you'll meet the young of most European countries, Japan, Africa, India and the USA.

Forth & Clyde Canal
Ranger on duty

FORTH and CLYDE
& UNION CANALS

Created originally as industrial arteries for central Scotland, these waterways were superseded by roads; so, for half a century their lengths languished out of use, becoming quiet green corridors colonised by plants, attracting increasing numbers of wildlife and being enjoyed by locals. The less salubrious bits are being cleaned up now and, thanks to the persistent enthusiasm of local communities and their refusal to let their canals moulder away, British Waterways are unlocking new potential through the great Millennium Project. Becoming more accessible to everyone, both canals are cared for and monitored by Canal Countryside Rangers.

Where the canal broadens to form basins, like at Firhill, you can learn windsurfing or canoeing. Along the towpaths, made for heavy horses to drag barges, you can cycle, run, or walk your dog. Sit by a lock in summer, contemplating the reflections, breathing in the scent of wildflowers and watching turquoise Damselflies glinting in the sunshine. And Firhill basin now has more interesting objects than shopping trolleys beneath its surface, thanks to regular clean-ups; the fishing's good both here, in the lesser-known silent stretches at Wyndford Lock and all the way to Falkirk. Artists find

Forth & Clyde Canal
Wyndford brambles

Forth & Clyde Canal
Wyndford fishers

a wonderful source of inspiration anywhere on the banks.

The Union Canal goes from Fountainbridge in Edinburgh, via Ratho and Broxburn to Falkirk Junction, then out to Grangemouth on the Forth and Clyde Canal. The Forth & Clyde Canal follows the Romans' Antonine Wall route westward, edging past Castlecary, Banknock, Kilsyth, Kirkintilloch, Bishopbriggs, snaking through Glasgow's poshest and poorest districts, past Spiers Wharf, Possilpark and Firhill on its way to pretty Bowling Basin and the Clyde.

All sorts of organisations use these waterways, like the Forth and Clyde Society, the Linlithgow Canal Society and the boat trip businesses at Kirkintilloch and Ratho.

There are two Canal Countryside Ranger Services, one looking after the east, covering the Forth, Falkirk, the Union Canal, Broxburn, West Lothian and Edinburgh, the other responsible for the western sections of the Forth and Clyde

The Union canal
reaches from
Fountainbridge in
Edinburgh to join with
the Forth & Clyde Canal
at Grangemouth.
A canal scene at Ratho

Canal. Both have been planting, increasing the vegetation along the water's edge. This will help banks cope with the wash from a growing number of boats which, by moving it about, will improve the quality of the water. Rangers link up with canal user groups, including schools and colleges. They work to improve water safety awareness among children and help them develop watery environmental projects.

There's also lots of heritage and historical interest, such as the famous Telford Aqueduct. With the Millennium Project comes a new wonder of engineering – the boat lift at Falkirk which conveys craft on a gigantic wheel from one canal to the other (they're at different heights here) without the need for locks. New visitor centres, tearooms and hostels are coming onstream, with fleets of floating classrooms and a programme of open day events. Volunteers are aiming to help disabled people enjoy boat trips.

Although access is good for walkers, some of the towpaths are too narrow for horses, so a trial horse-riding section is being investigated.

Bike riders, however, have lots of scope. Sustrans Glasgow to Edinburgh route uses the old Airdrie-Bathgate railway, leading onto the Union Canal towpath, with links south-east to Musselburgh, north to the Forth Road Bridge and westward to Loch Lomond and Ardrossan.

Bikers on the Forth & Clyde Canal at Firhill

Vital Spark at Crinan

GLASGOW & **THE WEST**

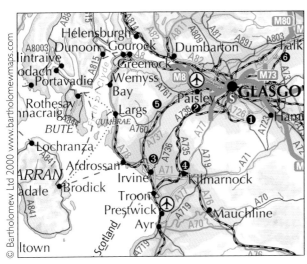

1. Calderglen Country Park
2. Gleniffer Braes Country Park
3. Eglinton Country Park
4. Dean Castle Country Park
5. Muirshiel Regional Park
6. Palacerigg Country Park

INFORMATION
OS Map Nos 62 – 64, 68 – 71, 76

LOCAL AUTHORITIES

Glasgow City Council, City Chambers, George Square, GLASGOW G2 1DU Tel 0141 287 2000

East Ayrshire Council, Council Headquarters, London Road, KILMARNOCK Tel 01563 576000

East Dunbartonshire Council, Tom Johnston House, Civic Way, Kirkintilloch, GLASGOW G66 4TJ Tel 0141 578 8000

East Renfrewshire Council, Eastwood Park, Giffnock, GLASGOW G46 6UG Tel 0141 577 3000

Inverclyde Council, Clyde Square, Municipal Buildings, GREENOCK PA15 1LY Tel 01475 717171

North Ayrshire Council, Cunninghame House, Friar's Croft, Irvine KA12 8EE Tel 01294 324100

North Lanarkshire Council, Civic Centre, Motherwell ML1 1TW Tel 01698 302222

Renfrewshire Council, Cotton Street, PAISLEY PA1 1LE Tel 0141 842 5000

South Ayrshire Council, Wellington Square, Ayr KA7 1DR Tel 01292 612000

South Lanarkshire Council, Almada Street, Hamilton ML3 0AA Tel 01698 454444

West Dunbartonshire Council, Garshake Road, Dumbarton G82 3PU Tel 01389 737000

TOURIST INFORMATION CENTRES

GLASGOW TIC Tel 0141 204 4400

ABINGTON Tel 01864 502436

BIGGAR Tel 01899 221066

GLASGOW AIRPORT Tel 0141 848 4440

Hundreds of miles of footpaths, cycle paths and riverside walkways radiate from Glasgow's centre. Beyond lie countless lochs and canals to boat and fish on, and stretches of accessible countryside to explore. West of the Central Belt, people are indeed well-provided with places to escape from their city. Country Parks welcome visitors and locals, like the two big Regional Park areas, all complete with Countryside Ranger services and loads of nature and wildlife to enjoy, mostly for free.

GREENOCK Tel 01475 722007

HAMILTON Tel 01698 285590

LANARK Tel 01555 661661

PAISLEY Tel 0141 889 0711

AYRSHIRE & ARRAN
Tel 01292 317 696

AYR Tel 01292 288688

BRODICK, Isle of Arran
Tel 01770 302140/302401

IRVINE Tel 01294 313886

KILMARNOCK
Tel 01563 539090

LARGS Tel 01475 673765

MILLPORT (Seasonal)
Tel 01475 530735

BUTE Tel 01700 502151

COUNTRY PARKS, ESTATES AND RANGER SERVICES

CALDERGLEN COUNTRY
PARK Visitor Centre
Tel 01355 236644

DRUMPELLIER COUNTRY
PARK Tel 01236 422257

EGLINTON COUNTRY PARK
Tel 01294 551776

DEAN CASTLE COUNTRY
PARK Tel 01563 522702
Countryside Ranger Service
Tel 01563 574916
Riding Centre
Tel 01563 541123

Woodroad Park
Tel 01563 574916

MOUNT STUART (Seasonal)
Tel 01700 503877
Scotrail inclusive package
Glasgow – Mount Stuart
Tel 0345 484950

GLENIFFER BRAES COUNTRY
PARK Tel 0141 884 3794

POLLOK COUNTRY PARK
Countryside Ranger Centre
Tel 0141 632 9299
Country Park Manager
Tel 0141 632 9299
Burrell Collection
Tel 0141 287 2550
Pollok House Tel 0141 616
6410

LINN PARK Tel 0141 637 1147
Equitation Centre
Tel 0141 637 3096

Each local authority gives its own particular emphasis. North Lanarkshire looks after Strathclyde Regional Park, with watersports galore. Palacerigg is famous for its collection of animals, South Lanarkshire's Chatelherault for its vast woods and beautiful visitor centre. West Dunbartonshire has Leven Valley, while East Dunbartonshire's Mugdock has a history going back to Robert the Bruce.

Calderglen Country Park's eight miles of nature trails take you along wooded river banks, with waterfalls and interesting geology. Your kids can let off steam on energy-intensive adventure play areas, or contemplate the goats in the little zoo. There's a Special Needs play area too. Annual events like the Country Fair and a Classic Automobile Rally add to regular happenings run by the Countryside Rangers. With the Rangers, try orienteering, photographing flowers, children's hikes or water divining. Enter a family pet show, or enjoy aromatherapy. Older folk enjoy the warm conservatory, the seats around the formal gardens and aviaries nearby, and there's a courtyard with shop, tearoom and Visitor Centre not far from the main car park.

Drumpellier Country Park has the Monkland Canal, play areas, woodland walks, a Visitor Centre, café, loos, nursery and butterfly house on the shore of Lochend Loch and convenient car-parking. Here you can buy fishing permits, and hire boats in summer.

Further afield, Muirshiel Regional Park covers the western half of Renfrewshire and includes privately-run Kelburn Country Park. Near Paisley, Renfrewshire runs Gleniffer Braes. Travelling further down the Firth of Clyde, on the wilder north-west shore, Argyll Forest Enterprise is active, and everyone can enjoy the towpaths of the Crinan Canal. On the more heavily populated south side of the river there are several good Country Parks run by local authorities, private concerns and NTS. NTS manage the furthest south Country Parks at Culzean and Brodick Castles. Local authorities run Eglinton at Irvine, Dean Castle at Kilmarnock and Woodroad at Cumnock.

Eglinton Country Park is an elegant landscape, for centuries the seat of the Earls of Eglinton, now with ruined towers and pretty prospects. In early summer, walking through the flowering trees might inspire you to pen a lyrical poem. Wildlife flourishes along the peaceful riverside and around the loch, and Countryside Rangers help interpret what you see. They'll also teach you 'skills for the hills', work on increasing your fitness, take you on guided walks – and cycle runs. The Visitor Centre is near the car park and has a shop, tearoom, loos, and a play area.

Dean Castle Country Park is a delight. Originally the seat of the Boyd family, Earls of Kilmarnock, the castle houses a Discovery Room. This 200 acre estate is full of interest. Woodland walks lead you to various animal enclosures for Rare Breeds, Red Deer and the Riding Centre. Children have a safe Adventure Playground and a pond for feeding ducks. From March to September the Countryside Ranger service runs a full programme of weekend events, from mediaeval battle re-enactment to astronomy, treasure hunts to bog-celebrations, a dog show – and a Fairytale Walk. There's even a special Ranger Roadshow, and National Play Day seems like a good institution. Car-parking is a short distance away from the Visitor Centre, which has a tearoom, and loos are strategically-placed around the policies.

Working also at Woodroad Park, Dean Castle Rangers run an afternoon of 'Art in the Park'. And why not try the Irvine Valley Ramble, the Cycle Safari or the two-rivers walk along the Fenwick and Crawfurdland Waters.

Other places of interest include Finlaystone Estate, above Port Glasgow, and Mount Stuart, open in summer on the island of Bute, with its 18th century pinetum and its woodland habitats.

Useful countryside CD ROMS are beginning to appear; *Glasgow's Wildlife* details every green space, loch, bog and woodland around the city and in it you can easily find what grows, flies and runs about in them. Mugdock's *A Park For All Seasons* includes its history set against a musical

HOGGANFIELD LOCH
Tel 0141 632 9299

CATHKIN BRAES Info from Countryside Ranger at Linn Park Tel 0141 637 1147

TOLLCROSS COUNTRY PARK
Tel 0141 763 1863

DARNLEY MILL Tel 0141 632 9299

DAWSHOLM Tel 0141 632 9299

MUGDOCK COUNTRY PARK
Tel 0141 956 6100

CLYDE MUIRSHIEL
Tel 01505 614791
www.scottishpark.com

Lunderston Bay Picnic & Play Area
Tel 01475 521129

Muirshiel Centre & Country Park Tel 01505 842803

RSPB Nature Centre
Tel 01505 842663

CORNALEES BRIDGE CENTRE
Tel 01475 521458

CASTLE SEMPLE COUNTRY PARK Lochwinnoch
Tel 01505 842882
Castle Semple Watersports/Activity Centre Tel 01505 842882

Castle Semple Activities Centre, Lochwinnoch (Tel 01505 842882)

FINLAYSTONE ESTATE Langbank
Ranger Service Tel 01475 540505
Environmental and historical schools activities Tel 01475 540505

KELBURN COUNTRY CENTRE
Tel 01475 568685

CULZEAN CASTLE AND COUNTRY PARK
NTS Ranger Service/Visitor Centre Tel 01655 884400
Castle Tel 01655 884455

BRODICK CASTLE AND COUNTRY PARK Isle of Arran
Countryside Centre/Ranger Office Tel 01770 302462
Castle Tel 01770 302202

GOATFELL
NTS Tel 01770 302462

FOREST ENTERPRISE
Brodick Tel 01770 302218

STRATHCLYDE REGIONAL PARK
Tel 01698 266155

DALZIELL PARK Tel 01698 266155

CHATELHERAULT COUNTRY PARK Visitor Centre
Tel 01698 4262213

FALLS OF CLYDE, NEW LANARK AND NEW LANARK WORLD HERITAGE CENTRE
New Lanark Visitor Centre
Tel 01555 661345

PALACERIGG COUNTRY PARK
Cumbernauld
Tel 01236 720047
Palacerigg Golf Course
Tel 01236 721461
Countryside Craft Courses Tel 01236 720047

PUBLIC TRANSPORT

GLASGOW AIRPORT
Tel 0141 887 1111

PRESTWICK AIRPORT
Tel 01292 479822

SCOTRAIL Tel 0345 484950

BUSES
National Express
Tel 08705 808080
Stagecoach Glasgow
Tel 0141 333 1100
Ayr Tel 01292 613500
Brodick Tel 01770 302000
Cumnock Tel 01290 421930
Kilmarnock Tel 01563 525192
City Link (Bookings and enquires
Tel 0990 50 50 50

FERRIES
Caledonian MacBrayne Ltd
Gourock Tel 01475 650100
Renfrew-Yoker Passenger Ferry
Tel 0141 885 2123

background, illustrated with watercolours, and there's loads of useful information about what you can do and find there.

With such a vast range of outdoor places available in the Glasgow area, people of all ages and stages of fitness are spoilt for choice. What follows are six samples of what's on offer.

Calderglen Country Park playground

Calderglen Country Park's annual Fair Day

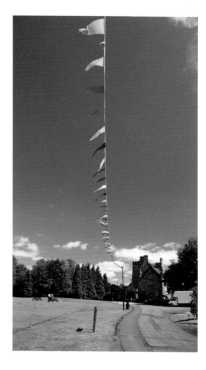

GLASGOW

Scotland's largest city Glasgow has spent centuries being a centre of international trade and industry. But the name means 'Dear Green Place' and its citizens enjoy 70 parks and access to a variety of waterways and lochs. Around Glasgow you really can get active out of doors.

Linn Park bridge and riders

You like walking? Sample the 10 mile walkway from Kelvingrove Park to Kirkintilloch – or the nearby Forth and Clyde canal towpath. Cyling? Cross the Clyde by Bell's Brig and head north to Loch Lomond, west to the Clyde coast, south to link in with the National Cycle Network, or eastward to Edinburgh and beyond, all on well-maintained Sustrans cycle-paths.

Go birdwatching at peaceful Hogganfield Loch, or feed the swans – Glasgow's first-ever pair were a gift from Shakespeare's Stratford. Search for blue butterflies on Cathkin Braes above Castlemilk or visit Pollok, for 700 years the wealthy Maxwell family's estate, now a Country Park for everyone.

Glasgow City Council Ranger services have their HQ at Pollok and satellite centres at Linn and Tollcross parks. There's a new Environment Centre open at Tollcross complete with Rangers, though you might spot this particular species organising events or monitoring wildlife around any of Glasgow's green habitats.

Bluebells in Eglinton Country Park

Pollok Country Park sits by the White Cart River 3 miles from the city centre, surrounded by motorway and urban sprawl. 361 acres of woodland, formal gardens, parkland and policies, it contains the Burrell Museum, Pollok House

The White Cart River in Pollock Country Park

and three convenient car-parks. Yet, wander its peaceful paths listening to the birds and the occasional moo from the fold of Highland cattle, breathe in the perfume of its bluebell woods – and you'll forget urban stress.

Look in to the Visitor Centre, beside the Old Stable Courtyard, with its regularly updated 'Recent Wildlife Sightings' board – there's usually a Countryside Ranger to talk to. See a Wildlife Garden in action – this one's ten years old. Along the river, look for the flash of a blue Kingfisher – even Otter, mink or Roe Deer might honour you with an appearance. At nightfall Pippistrelle Bats fly, Tawny Owls hoot – and Foxes go hunting.

Join one of Pollok's clubs. The Young Naturalists group enthuses children about environmental issues. The Junior Rangers club gives teenagers a great outdoors time, and there's a lively 50+ Club. Everyone enjoys Autumn Edible sessions and other sociable happenings. Occasionally, heavy horses may be on hand to pull you through the park on a cart, and there's a wonderful Family Day in August.

Further up the White Cart, Linn is Glasgow's second

Feeding the ducks at Hogganfield Loch

largest park and has interesting links with nearby Netherton Braes and Cathkin Braes. With no internal car-parks, it's safe for toddlers and dogs, but a longish walk to the Visitor Centre (not always manned). A good programme of events and activities is organised from here. With the monthly Dipper Club, 8 – 12's might be investigating the mysteries of flight, life in the rainforest, star-gazing, or planting trees. Teenagers might be letting off steam rhodie-bashing. Adults can join Conservation Volunteers here. Dogs enjoy running free, only being put on leashes in the courtyard where there's an Equestrian Centre.

Cycling in Pollock Country Park

Woodland clothes the riverbank, providing shelter for both resident and migrating birds. There are Dippers and Dunnock, Chiffchaffs and Willow Warblers, some identifiable by their sounds, if you know how – and there's an expert to guide you. Imagine finding a lone Heron fishing here in the town. You can fish, too. Ask the Countryside Rangers about permits. Or simply enjoy a good walk by the riverside, part of a walkway planned from Eaglesham down to the Clyde at Renfrew. It is steep in places, though, so not recommended for wheels.

Learning about the countryside

MUGDOCK COUNTRY PARK

This magnificent Country Park was the ancient domain of the Gallant Graham clan. You can still see their ruined castles, Mugdock and Craigend, but now their 740 acres are open to all of us. There's a wealth of wildlife and history to discover, and lots for everyone to do – you can even become your own sundial. Craigends Stable Courtyard houses a tearoom (muddy boots welcome), craft workshops, loos and the Countryside Ranger Service. There are two nearby play areas and two bookable covered barbecue sites.

For a feeling that you're far more than 10 miles from the heart of Glasgow, walk Peitches Moor, or Kyber Fields where cattle graze contentedly. In Spring, wander through the bluebells, or ancient Mugdock Wood with the sun filtering through leaves, or contemplate the reflections on Mugdock Loch. In Autumn, meander among the mushrooms, or experience nightlife among the bats. Who was hanged on Gallowhill? Where is the Echo Stone, the Fairy Foxglove? What is a Blue Germander? And how will you recognise the Beastly Backswimmer?

Mugdock is at the heart of a great network of local footpaths. The West Highland Way passes through (see Heart of Scotland). Find paths for jogging and walking, with well-made boardwalks over boggy bits. Take your horse or your bike over specially laid-out trails. If you ride a wheelchair, book (free) a variety of motorised buggies – or persuade a cycling pal to do his rickshaw act with you on the new Duet. You'll find hard-surfaced paths leading from car parks, including one conveniently near Craigends Stables and a Walled Garden Centre.

Mugdock Wood and walkers – no more that 10 miles from the centre of Glasgow

Annual happenings include the Summer Fair, Mugdock Music Festival which brings together local musicians, Mugdock Superdog, when you can parade your pet, the Horticultural Fair, and Doors Open Day when you can enter the portals of Mugdock Castle.

Countryside Rangers work and give illustrated talks here and around East Dunbartonshire. Get up early in May for the Sunrise Songsters session on International Dawn Chorus Day, followed by a hearty tearoom breakfast. Then go pond-dipping – you might even net the Beastly Backswimmer. Have a go at orienteering. Take your model boat for a float, or your kite for a flight – after you've made them. Make a bird table. See if you're any good with a mediaeval longbow. There's a video theatre operating most weekend afternoons showing nature and countryside films and a Discovery Room for hands-on Nature experiences. 'Mugdock Moles' is the children's nature club and adults are welcomed by Mugdock's Conservation Volunteers.

The estate's history goes back to the 13th century, when Sir David Graham was a supporter of Robert the Bruce, and its most famous Graham was James, 5th Earl of Montrose (1612 – 1650). Nowadays, over 300,000 visitors a year enjoy its freedom and fresh air. On a sunny summer's day Craigend Stable courtyard can be busy, but you'll always find quiet spots further afield.

Muirshiel trees and Misty Law

MUIRSHIEL
& WEST RENFREWSHIRE

Rural west Renfrewshire has lots of scope for outdoor activity. Muirshiel Regional Park lies between Lochwinnoch and the Clyde, and a privately-owned Country Park, Finlaystone, adds to the amenity. Thanks to Sustrans (who welcome volunteers to help maintain their paths) cyclists have access to the area. Fit walkers might head for the summit of Misty Law or go orienteering. Water people kayak, sail and windsurf on Castle Semple Loch. Skill-learning includes raft building, archery and – bodging?

Lunderston Bay sand castles

Muirshiel is 102 square miles of truly accessible moorland, lochs, rivers and woodland, employing 70 experts; sports coaches and Countryside Rangers plus the only Special Needs Ranger in Scotland. The Kilbarchan HQ runs three Visitor Centres; Cornalees Bridge, Muirshiel itself and Castle Semple Loch, all have nearby car-parks and are open, including loos, from April to Autumn.

Cornalees Bridge Rangers use Lunderston Bay for seaside learning experiences and their annual Victorian Picnic, complete with sand-castle contests, always draws the crowds. Walk the People Trail through local history all the way back to the Romans, the Vikings and Iron Age Wo/ Man.

Prehistoric Castle Semple Loch was the

River Clyde, till a massive upheaval in the earth's crust. Now the Loch harbours freshwater fish, an RSPB Nature Centre and boats. Don't let disability stop you learning watersports, the centre's equipped. Find out if you have a hidden talent for dousing. Try Special Needs Cycle Day, or Walk with Witches.

Question; What are Terraformers? Answer; Muirshiel's environmental nature club for 8 – 14s. Adults can cycle through industrial history, tune in to natural rhythms, brush up on their broom-making skills, hike over the hills to Largs, listen to Midsummer larks – the list is endless. But up here, high on the moors, why not simply walk for miles and breathe in great gusts of heathery fresh air. The wide skies and sheer sense of space are balm to the soul.

Kelburn Castle and Country Centre is part of Muirshiel Regional Park

Exploring historic Finlaystone won't cost you much. Currently the seat of Clan Macmillan, this 140 acre estate perches high above the Clyde. You'll be following in the footsteps of John Knox and Robert Burns as you explore its mixed woodland or revel in its spectacular springtime drifts of daffodils, bluebells and snowdrops. Children – of all ages – enjoy the play areas, picnic and barbecue sites. Try the bird hide, the pond-dipping platforms, the wayfaring course, or walk the curly Celtic pavement. The canine estate residents don't object to visiting dogs running freely through their woods – and may even join in their games. But if you're looking for tranquillity, wander through 10 acres of formal gardens, past a magnificent herbaceous border, seen against a backdrop of the river and distant mountains.

Some areas are accessible to wheelchair users

Countryside Rangers help visitors, and maintain the footpaths. Car parking is near the Visitor Centre, shop, loos and a fascinating museum of dolls collected from all over the world, and there' s a tearoom.

Culzean Castle has 17 miles of
walks through formal gardens
and woodland, along clifftop
and shore

The 13 acre Swan Pond is
Culzean's most famous
landscape feature, usually full of
water-fowl

CULZEAN CASTLE & BRODICK CASTLE COUNTRY PARKS

Culzean and Brodick Castles, each unique in their way, both benefit from the loving care of NTS. At Culzean, 17 miles of walks weave through a rich diversity of habitats. In season you'll find wild garlic, bluebells, snowdrops, daffodils and foxgloves in their thousands and you might see Roe Deer or Red Squirrel. Otters sometimes play along the shorelines. The park is bounded by the walkable old Kennelmount railway and its Glenside station is now a caravan and camping site.

Wander down a wildflower-bedecked path to discover tiny Port Carrick beach. Walk back along the cliff path, and you'll come across strategically-placed seats with views, just when you need a rest. Further inland, visit the Herb Garden and the Deer Park. Lovely at all times of year, Culzean, Scotland's first Country Park, opened in 1967, is spectacular in Spring and early summer when the huge collection of mature Rhododendrons and Azaleas are in bloom. Because of its wide variety of deciduous trees, autumn's also colourful.

Culzean Castle sits on a volcanic cliff-edge promontory, which in ancient times sheltered cave-dwellers. From the 12th century it was a stronghold; belonging to the Kennedys, associated with Bruce, its 16th century keep was extended in the 18th century by Robert Adam.

Level paths lead from a car park to Culzean's capacious courtyard Visitor Centre, with information, loos, shops, a restaurant, exhibitions, and a Countryside Ranger base where there's usually someone on duty. These Rangers also run a Young Naturalists' Club.

Visible from Culzean, the island of Arran has been inhabited since neolithic times. There Brodick Castle, seat

Sweeping across the Arran hillside, way-marked trails take you through a complete microcosm of the Scottish Highlands, for NTS also owns the neighbouring 6,500 acres that include Glen Rosa and Goatfell

Brodick Ranger Centre suits all ages

of the Dukes of Hamilton since the 13th century, is surrounded by the only island-based Country Park in the UK. Annual fun includes International Bog Day, and Search and Rescue Day, complete with helicopter.

Brodick Castle's Countryside Rangers have huge scope here, working from seashore to mountain tops through woodland and open hillside. Try a Monday afternoon Ranger Ramble as an introduction, or Thursday's Watery Wild Life explorations of seashore and freshwater pond. Wilma's Walk is good for those with visual impairment or who have Special Needs and there's an electric buggy available. There's lots to do for youngsters – and an adventure playground. All the local 13 yr-olds on the island spend 3 days here on environmental studies and some return for Work Experience. You can join a ten day Thistle Camp and really leave your mark on the landscape here.

This excellent Ranger service operates from a Countryside Centre within the park, with good facilities for groups. It's well worth dropping in to their Display Room to read the daily natural hot news. Take a peek at the summits through the public binocular before setting forth.

The Goatfell Ranger's guided walks tackle a different peak each week. Hugely knowledgable, she also sees to footpath repair, bog restoration and the biological monitoring that, for instance, sets the cull numbers for deer control.

An antique bus will deliver you to the car park from the ferry terminal. It's quite a steep walk up via the pay desk and a flight of steps to the terrace on which the Castle is built – but great views when you get there – and disabled people can park nearer. There's a wildlife garden, a shop, tearoom, and loos.

photo: Bob Reid

Watersports at Strathclyde
Country Park

STRATHCLYDE REGIONAL PARK & CHATELHERAULT COUNTRY PARK

Strathclyde and Chatelherault are geographically close, but couldn't be more different in origin, or in what they have to offer.

With a loch at its heart, Strathclyde is one of the most active Country Parks in Scotland for outdoor recreation and environmental education. Created from a post-industrial bog, in one of the most courageous land-reclamation schemes ever, its 1100 acres now add immeasurably to the local amenity, hosting a year-round programme of events from international rowing and sailing regattas, horse shows, football and hockey matches, to country fairs and leisure exhibitions.

Wander 20 miles of well-maintained footpaths through the varied habitats of woodland, wetland and open parkland, enjoy horse-riding over 7 miles of bridle paths, cycle, row, or fish. Enjoy simply skiddling in the water or sunbathing, along the tranquil eastern shore. Feed the swans, or watch the abundant wildlife – 170 species of birds have come to

Planting primroses

photo: Bob Reid

photo: Bob Reid

Strathclyde pond dipping

Strathclyde winter sports

photo: Bob Reid

breed here. Hire boating equipment or bring and paddle your own canoe. Safety is a priority so there's always a rescue boat on duty. If you prefer to take your exercise indoors, try the gym – but for a sense of freedom, set off along the River Clyde Walkway, which passes through the Park.

Strathclyde's dedicated team of Countryside Rangers organise year-round events. Explore the mysteries of 80 'ologies', learn how to navigate hills and towns, go on a nature treasure trail, design and make your own kite, or bat box, try orienteering or visit nearby Dalziell.

Children can head for several play areas or a broad sandy beach, safe for the bucket and spade brigade. And there's the controversial (noisy) theme park where, on a green caterpillar, you zoom through holes in a gigantic red apple. Environmentally educational?

History buffs enjoy exploring the remains of a Roman bathhouse, or reflecting on the Battle of Bothwell Brig (1679) which put an end to 400 Covenanters, slain right here.

Stay in the park in hotels, caravan or camping sites. Enjoy its restaurants and bars. Car-parks are strategically placed so that you can select any area for your outing whether you're able-bodied or not. Disappointingly, local advice is to avoid the more secluded car parks after dusk, and during daylight if you're a lone walker or with children.

From Strathclyde you can see the elegant façade of Chatelherault looking down on Hamilton. Once the Duke of Hamilton's summer palace, it collapsed due to coal mining. Recently restored, it's now pretty enough to host your wedding. Posh ducal hounds' kennels house an

Chatelerhault looks down on the town of Hamilton

excellent Visitor Centre with Countryside Ranger service, museum displays, gift shop, loos and café.

Once part of Cadzow Forest hunting grounds, beloved of medieval Scottish kings, Chatelherault's grounds have become a lovely Country Park.

Treat yourself to a Ranger-guided walk through important native woodland. Tramp the Avon Walkway and see the spectacularly deep gorge, its river swirling below the ruins of Cadzow Castle. Look for coal on the Hole Story Trail. Try the 6 mile Green Bridge Trail, or surprise yourself on the shorter Deer Park Trail by finding not deer, but cows – the rare white Cadzow Cattle, still crowned with horns. Go far enough and you'll find yourself in a secret green grove of ancient Cadzow Oak trees, old enough to have sheltered the Druids, each tree with its own distinct personality and, you get the feeling, with plenty to say. The atmosphere here is palpable.

Other Chatelherault interests include the adventure playground, the picnic and barbecue sites and a good garden centre. You can park a short walk from the house, closer if you're disabled. Cyclists are welcome on the tarmac trails, but the rest are for walkers.

Palacerigg treetop walk

PALACERIGG COUNTRY PARK

As you enter the posh-looking portals of Palacerigg, the first thing you see is a lot of animals. Bison lumber about the first field, deer munch grass daintily across the way. Snowy Owls stare unblinkingly at you, Mink scuttle away, Pine Marten hide, Lynx and Wildcats flaunt their figures in the sunshine, the cuddly-looking Arctic Foxes curl up, Reindeer rub their antlers red – and if you go far enough you'll find wolves lurking about ripping up raw meat beneath the trees. But there's far more to this Country Park than Rare Breeds and caged beasts, though this does indeed represent a well cared-for and important collection of Scottish and European creatures.

Once a bleak upland farm, now really wild wildlife flourishes freely among its native trees and shrubs, a sanctuary for thriving populations of Badgers, Hares, wild Roe Deer and a great variety of birds. Tiptoe up the Treetop Walkway to watch the high flyers, or potter around the pond to admire the aquabatics of the watery ones, including two very stately black swans that look like Queen Victoria with lipstick on. Up on Fannyside Moor you might find rare Bean Geese feeding.

Visit the well-equipped Countryside Ranger Centre and their Display Room to discover what's about. Use the audio-visual displays and try the hands-on interactive panels. Book

Experts run weekend Country Craft courses on such things as papermaking, wood carving, weaving and dyeing, stick making, beekeeping, charcoal burning, willow sculpture, basket-making, and chainsaw sculpture, all run from the unique home-grown timber Millennium Longhouses

a place on a guided walk, perhaps to Broadwood Loch, or go treeplanting for the Millennium. Learn how to fish St Maurice's Pond. Ramble with the Romans – and the navvies – along the Antonine Wall and the Forth and Clyde Canal. At the annual July Country Fair, see sheep being shorn, horses being shod and have a go at some ancient crafts yourself. You can even learn to make woodland music with your own xylophone, flute or drum. Join in the Family Fun Day in August, with its pony rides, jugglers, games and competitions.

The Badger Set is Palacerigg's nature club. There's a playground, an aerial runway and a farmyard full of sheep, ducks, goats – and cheery children chasing chickens. Peacocks look on disdainfully, trailing their fancy tails.

Leave your dog at home as this Country Park is not suitable, but for horse-riders there's an 8 mile network of bridle paths. Walkers have nature trails to wander, through moorland, grassland and woods and there's historic interest too, from peat cutting at Gobhar to evidence of fireclay mining at Glencryan.

You get a good bowl of soup and other tasteful treats in Palacerigg's tearoom. Level paths lead to the Visitor Centre – and loos – from the nearby car park. But perhaps the most unforgettably hilarious activities at Palacerigg is their Halloween event, with a new script every year. Don't miss it.

photo: Malcolm Fife

This view of Salisbury Crags in
Edinburgh's Holyrood Park is
taken from the Dumbiedykes
area and is literally yards from
the city centre

EDINBURGH &
the LOTHIANS

© Bartholomew Ltd 2000 www.bartholomewmaps.com

INFORMATION
OS Map Nos 65 – 67, 73, 74

LOCAL AUTHORITIES

East Lothian Council, Council
Buildings, Court Street, Haddington
Tel 01620 827827

Edinburgh City Council,
10 Waterloo Place, Edinburgh
Tel 0131 200 2000

Midlothian Council, Buccleuch
Street, Dalkeith
Tel 0131 270 75000

West Lothian Council, Almondvale
Boulevard, Livingston
Tel 01506 77000

TOURIST INFORMATION CENTRES

Edinburgh & the Lothians
Tel 0131 473 3800
Website www.edinburgh.org

Dunbar Tel 01368 863353

Linlithgow (Seasonal)
Tel 01506 844600

Newtongrange (Seasonal)
Tel 0131 663 4262

North Berwick Tel 01620 892197

Old Craighall Tel 0131 653 6172

Penicuik (Seasonal)
Tel 01968 673846

COUNTRYSIDE RANGER SERVICES

City of Edinburgh Ranger Service
Tel 0131 447 7145
Web site
www.cecrangerservice.demon.co.uk

Almondell & Calderwood Country
Park Tel 01506 461118

Almond Valley Heritage Trust
Tel 01506 414957

Beecraigs Country Park
Tel 01506 844516

East Lothian District Ranger Service
Tel 01620 824161

East Lothian Council Ranger Service
Tel 01620 827318/827845/827423
Hermitage of Braid, Edinburgh
Tel 0131 447 7145

Edinburgh is one of the beautiful cities of the world. Princes Street Gardens is at its heart and from that famous landmark Edinburgh Castle, the Old Town tumbles down its Royal Mile of ridgeback rock to Holyrood Palace, all set against dramatic red Salisbury Crags.

Edinburgh folk have green places aplenty to wander in; the Meadows and Holyrood Park are in town; parks and rivers lead outwards to the Lothian countryside. Set between the Forth estuary and the Pentland hills, the

John Muir Country Park
Tel 01620 860556

Muiravonside Country Park
Tel 01506 845311

Pentland Hills Regional Park
Tel 0131 445 3383

Historic Scotland Ranger Service
Tel 0131 556 2042
Tel 0131 556 1761

HOLYROOD PARK Information
Centre and Ranger Service
Tel/Fax 0131 556 1761

HOPETOUN HOUSE
Tel 0131 331 2451

WESTER HAILES
Ranger Service Tel 0131 458 5043

POLKEMMET COUNTRY PARK
The Park Centre Whitburn
Tel 01501 743905

VOGRIE COUNTRY PARK
Nr Gorebridge
Ranger Service Tel 0875 821990

DALKEITH COUNTRY PARK
Ranger Service Tel 0131 654 1666
or 0131 663 5684
Buccleuch Countryside Service
Tel 01848 331555
Dalkeith – Penicuik Walkway
Tel 0131 654 1666

DUNBAR AND JOHN MUIR
COUNTRY PARK
Tel 01368 863886
Barns Ness
Tel 01368 863536

PENTLAND HILLS REGIONAL
PARK Ranger Service
Tel 0131 445 3383
Bonaly Country Park
Tel 0131 445 3383

MIDLOTHIAN SKI CENTRE
Tel 0131 445 4433

Lothians are full of Country Parks and woodland in which everyone is welcome. There are at least ten lochs, like Rosebery Reservoir, there are waterways like the Union Canal and the Rivers Tyne, Esk and Almond, and there are accessible walkways through private estates as well. There's also improving scope for horse riders and cyclists.

Pentland Hills Regional Park is a wonderful resource right on the city's doorstep. Midlothian dry ski slope at Hillend is a well-known facility, but there's more to these steeply rising hills than skiing. Although, like other Regional Parks in Scotland, much of the land here is privately owned and full of working farms which still support a rural community, there's a long tradition of co-operation with farmers, and public access. There's a diversity of wildlife habitats, and the geology is interesting. Bonaly Country Park makes a good starting point for hillwalking.

West Lothian is particularly well-served with Country Parks. Calderwood follows tributaries down to join the River Almond in Almondell Country Park, giving people from Livingston, Broxburn and the Calders breathing space. Having been a working area, there's lots of industrial archaeology for you to see; bridges, gas works and an old mill, as well as woodland walks and a great programme of events for everyone.

Beecraigs and Muiravonside Country Parks surround the south side of Linlithgow and have animals, domestic and wild, a wide variety of landscapes, and lots of activities to try.

Polkemmet Country Park is the furthest west. An old estate, its 68 acres offer you wooded policies and grazing land to wander, picnic places, children's play areas, a restaurant and loos. There's also golf, a driving range, putting and bowls.

East Lothian has the John Muir Country Park and several Nature Reserves along its coastline. People are discouraged from disturbing sanctuaries kept for migrating

Edinburgh Castle

PUBLIC TRANSPORT

Traveline
(one stop info details of local transport)
Tel 0800 23 23 23 (local calls)
Tel 0131 225 3858 (national calls)
Lothian Region Transport
0131 554 4494
City Link 0990 505050
First Bus Enquiries
0131 663 1945
Guide Friday 0131 556 2244

Edinburgh Airport
Tel 0131 333 1000

Scotrail Tel 0345 484950

or over-wintering birds, but here and there you'll find human-friendly places from which you can watch them. The Lammermuir Hills are full of inland, geological, historical and archaeological interest, as well as being great walking and cycling country.

Vogrie is a compact Country Park with something for everyone and a pretty Victorian mansion at its centre. Countryside Rangers based here travel far and wide around Midlothian, taking guided walks and working with conservation volunteer groups.

The Lothians and Edinburgh are well-served with breathing spaces and scope for outdoor activity. Take a look at the following samples of what's available.

Chesnut flowers in Midlothian's Vogrie Country Park

CITY OF EDINBURGH

Everyone can find walking spaces in and around Edinburgh, and there are lots of outdoor activities to try. You can enter the city by boat, on foot or by bike if you don't fancy public transport. The Clyde Forth Cycle route is one of several in the Edinburgh area and Sustrans plan more. But first of all, Edinburgh our capital city is about hills and history.

Edinburgh Castle, a stronghold since 1,000 BC, overlooks all the landscapes from the Forth to the Pentland Hills. Built on the core of an extinct volcano, its shape was reflected in a loch till Victorian engineers drained it to build Waverley Station. Calton Hill looks down Princes Street and behind it all the Salisbury Crags pile up towards another hill.

From its 12th century beginnings, Hermitage of Braid has had a mixed bag of residents. William Dick, a 17th century Provost of Edinburgh was one. Oliver Cromwell used it as a camp-site and Bonnie Prince Charlie plundered it. In more recent times it became a Boy Scouts' hostel. Now its pleasant landscape is open to everyone, wild birds and animals included. Edinburgh's Countryside Rangers are based here and they organise a wonderfully diverse programme of activities and events.

Their leaflets will inspire you to try lots of walks in the district. A particularly lovely one, through Dalmeny Estate, goes between Hawes Inn at South Queensferry and Cramond, where the River Almond spills into the Forth. At Cramond there was a Roman fort from 140 AD. Any day of the year you might find a 280 million year-old scallop fossil,

photo: Malcolm Fife

Duddingston Loch

in summer look for unusual butterflies. Waders and seabirds feed near Eagle Rock, out in the estuary look for Porpoise or Dolphin, nearer in, Shelduck. Hound Point has great views all the way from Edinburgh to the Trossachs, and at low tide you can cross the causeway to Cramond Island for a different view.

Historic Scotland's Ranger Service looks after the 640 acre Holyrood Park, once a royal hunting ground. Visitors love to climb the old volcano that is Arthur's Seat (820 ft), walk the Radical Road below the red cliffs of Salisbury Crags, or go bird-watching around the lochs. Duddingston Loch usually has parents and toddlers flinging lumps of bread to literally dozens of swans, ducks and geese. St Margaret's Loch, just below St Anthony's Chapel, also has swans and high on the hillside sits lonely wee Dunsapie Loch.

One of Edinburgh's secret pleasances is the Water of Leith. This useful little river trickles from the Colzium Springs up in the Pentland Hills, tumbles for 24 miles through Balerno, Juniper Green and Colinton, runs under the Dean Bridge, on to Stockbridge and scooshes out into the Forth at Leith. Once used for flushing industrial effluent away, it's no longer a repository for junk. In fact so much has it recovered, thanks to the efforts of local people, that it's now a designated Urban Wildlife Site. You're welcome to walk most of its length and Water of Leith Conservation Trust has produced a leaflet to guide you. Keep your eyes open for Otter on the Currie to Slateford stretch, Kingfisher between Roseburn and Stockbridge, brown trout, yellow flag Iris, greenfinch, and bank voles. Mind you – leeches lurk in yonder mud.

All sorts of interesting environmental and recreational projects are ongoing around Edinburgh, across the spectrum of ages, abilities and communities, such as the Green Belt Trust and Leap 21. Join the Nest Box scheme co-ordinated by the Ranger Service to help provide houses for birds or bats. Engage in communal Bulb or Tree Planting sessions, find out how to survey your local wildlife – how close are you to your nearest fox family? You might be surprised what near neighbours you are – maybe you're even sharing a dustbin. Tidy-minded? Then join in litter-picking or burn-clearance days – and socialise at the same time. You might come across future friends – or ghosts from Edinburgh's past.

Feeding the deer at Beecraigs Country Park

WEST LOTHIAN
BEECRAIGS & MUIRAVONSIDE
COUNTRY PARKS

Beecraigs is all woodland and water and open spaces, whilst Muiravonside has an industrial and historic background. Both have farms, good Countryside Ranger services and lots to see and do.

At Beecraigs, you have a grand 913 acres of freedom. Start at the Park Centre where you'll find lots of positive leaflets and useful info on fishing permits, pony permits, orienteering maps, hiring barbecue sites, camping and more. There's a Junior Rangers Club for 8–12s, and five car parks ranged around the park for easy access. Don't be put off by Beecraigs' fondness for negativity. Walking around, you'll keep seeing notices telling you what not to do – mostly things you wouldn't have thought of doing anyway. The overkill's endearingly funny.

Reasonably fit? Walk up Cockleroy Hill (Hill of Kings, 912 ft) for its great views from Arran's Goat Fell to the Forth's Bass Rock. Woodland walking, look for squirrels, rabbits and Tawny Owls. And don't get a fright if you hear a grunt. Rare pigs snuffle among the beech mast.

If you like fishing you're in luck, for there's a trout farm. Investigate the Rainbow's life-cycle, or recycle a trout yourself – catch one for tea on Beecraigs Loch. Don't go in August if the loch's stained with blooms of blue-green algae, which smell yeuchy.

Feed deer with the Countryside Rangers on pre-booked Deer Farm Walks. From the viewing platform watch these

Newparks Farm at Muiravonside with its great collection of animals is especially good to visit

peaceable (and, yes, tasty) creatures for hours; any sudden movement sends a shimmer of nerves through the herd like the wind through barley but, relaxed, they mew and whicker softly to each other, making one of the world's most tranquillising sounds.

Another gentle pleasure is wandering Balvernie Meadow seeking Mountain Pansies, Butterfly Orchids or Tormentil, counting the moths and butterflies and listening to the bees buzzing around Beecraigs.

Muiravonside is an 800 year-old estate. Once self-sufficient, now with added ash bing and coalfield railway, together it adds up to 170 acres of good Country Park for a day out. The River Avon flows through a deep, wooded gorge where, in Spring, you'll find bluebells, violets and primroses. Look for Badger, Fox and Roe Deer tracks and some of the 80 species of birds that live or pass through. Newparks farm is especially good to visit. It has a great collection of domestic animals old and young so it's fun for all ages.

Muiravonside estate's one-time owners, the adventurous Stirling family, helped found the SAS. Now the home farm makes a good Visitor Centre and Countryside Ranger base,

Highland cow at Muiravonside

with loos and a summer café. It's also interesting to explore the more industrial side of the park; old limekilns, a mill lade, even a mine shaft. Car parking is some distance from the Visitor Centre, but the walk is well surfaced. Controlled dogs are welcome here, but bring your pooper scooper.

There's scope for walking, both in and outwith Muiravonside. Ranger-led walks introduce you to little-known localities like Polmont Woods, Dorrator Bridge, Callendar Park and Kinneil Estate, the disused railways make level tracks and the Union Canal aqueduct is a famous piece of engineering heritage. Rangers might take you Bat watching, help you identify a food processor in the form of a Wandering Snail, discover the Golden-ringed Dragonfly they call a population controller, find a Springtail, or teach you crafts like papermaking. You might also find that grass has more to it than merely growing your lawn.

Amondell Visitor Centre

ALMONDELL, CALDERWOOD & POLKEMMET COUNTRY PARKS

Polkemmet, Calderwood and Almondell are old estates strung along the course of the River Almond. Today they provide West Lothian townsfolk with Country Parks and outdoor activities.

Polkemmet's 169 acres are well-served with car parks and loos and a good Information Centre. Children, including their disabled friends, enjoy its play area. There's a Fantasy Forest to give them fun plus a bit of knowledge about local nature. Polkemmet's Countryside Rangers lead various environmental events; woodland and riverside walks are there for you to wander, listening to the birds and keeping an eye open for a squirrel, rabbit or badger. Develop your golfing skills on the driving range, the putting green, or the neat nine-hole course – and afterwards picnic, book a barbecue, or patronise the restaurant and lounge bar.

Downriver, Almondell Country Park is connected to Calderwood and Oakbank by a walkway. Together, these three exemplify much that is good, and some things that are less good, about the present state of country parks in Scotland.

Almondell appears to approve of walkers, but makes car access difficult. If you're disabled, you're permitted to

The River Almond flows through the old estates of Polkemmet, Calderwood and Almondell

drive in to the Centre – after you've phoned to have the North Car Park entrance gate unlocked. Other drivers are stuck out on the periphery. First-time visitors arriving in the South Car Park, faced with a wall of seemingly impenetrable bushes, are left to guess which of the unsavoury-looking overgrown paths to risk plunging into, with neither welcoming notices nor maps to guide them. Asked about this, a Ranger explained loftily that Almondell was for locals and notice boards were placed where local walkers would see them. What – don't they welcome visitors or newcomers to this district?

That said, if you do persevere till your boots reach one of the well-made internal footpaths, you will find lovely walks through the woods and along the river. Enjoy spring flowers like Wood Anemones, bluebells and daffodils, in summer see glorious Rhododendrons and Azaleas in bloom, later wander through the warm woodland colours of autumn. Some path sections are steep, some have steps, but there are seats for stopping to admire the view – or catch your breath. Permeate the policies as far as the bustling stable-block Visitor Centre and you'll find people to talk to. You can picnic, or book a barbecue, and both Centre and loos are usefully open all year. Nearby you can still see some of the ornamental plantings done by the 18th century estate owner, Henry Erskine.

An imaginative Countryside Ranger service is based here, running the summer Look Group for 8–12s and tackling events, from the Great Egg Race at Easter to Christmas Crafts, Spring Clean sessions, an American Indian

Almondell humour

Day, a Poetry Picnic, an expedition to Linn's Mill Aqueduct, environmental Children's Challenge games and an interesting programme of guided walks. There's even a stone-skimming championship.

Calderwood once belonged to the Barons of Torpichen. You're advised to enter Calderwood from Gas Works Brae. Up the hill, Oakbank was a shale bing, left over from the mining industry, now left to return to nature. The threatening atmosphere is palpable here; creepy unlabelled paths dive into overhanging bushes. Flowers, lacewings and foxes might be doing all right up on unguarded Oakbank, but families and vulnerable people should definitely keep away.

On your bike, escape to explore the pleasant openness of the rest of West Lothian. There's a good set of leaflets and maps available listing cycling clubs and places you can buy spare parts. One 25 mile route links Livingston, West Calder and Bathgate using minor roads and new cycle tracks, taking you near Almond Valley's Heritage Centre and farm, a Vintage Bus Museum, and a Polkemmet detour. Excellent.

Rhododendron walk at
Vogrie Country Park

MIDLOTHIAN
VOGRIE & DALKEITH
COUNTRY PARKS

Dalkeith and Vogrie Country Parks are very different from each other, but together give Midlothian people a variety of outdoor experiences. Both have good Countryside Ranger services, which operate well beyond their boundaries.

Vogrie is a compact 260 acres of sweeping lawns, specimen trees, parkland, ponds, streams and woods. The whole estate is enclosed in belts of mixed woodland in which you can walk along lots of footpaths, and picnic in peace. The River Tyne wanders through the eastern edge, while a butterfly meadow graces the south side. There's a model railway, a walled garden and nursery, a curling pond and a Peace Garden. There's even a special house for Brownies. Inside the Victorian mansion, you'll find a Countryside Centre, audio-visual presentation, nature study centre, changing rooms and loos. Your wheelchair can access all of these – and the pleasant tea-room is open all year, though with restricted hours in winter.

Vogrie's Countryside Rangers, also based in the house, lead guided walks from six main sites around the district; Rosslyn Glen, Goreglen, Straiton Pond, Gladhouse Reservoir and the Penicuik Walkway, giving you a wide variety of habitats to explore. In summertime they run the popular Go Wild Week, in which 8–12s become enthused about survival. Very useful. Along with other Ranger services they work with conservation groups like Edinburgh's Green Team, and the environmental group Leap 21.

Dog walking at Vogrie is 'fairly relaxed' so long as your dog doesn't go eating toddlers or knocking old ladies down. If he does exhibit anti-social tendencies you will be asked to abide by the rules and leash him up.

Vogrie boasts a bookable 'flexi-field' for group fun and activities, and nine-hole golf course. There's an adventure

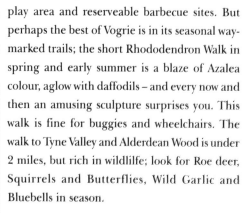

play area and reserveable barbecue sites. But perhaps the best of Vogrie is in its seasonal way-marked trails; the short Rhododendron Walk in spring and early summer is a blaze of Azalea colour, aglow with daffodils – and every now and then an amusing sculpture surprises you. This walk is fine for buggies and wheelchairs. The walk to Tyne Valley and Alderdean Wood is under 2 miles, but rich in wildlilfe; look for Roe deer, Squirrels and Butterflies, Wild Garlic and Bluebells in season.

Play at Vogrie

Dalkeith Country Park is part of the Buccleuch Estates mentioned in the Borders section. Here there's also lots to see and do. Find man-made caves and tunnels, enjoy parklands first enclosed for deer by Charles 1 in 1637, and wander through 18th and 19th century landscapes. Pause and admire the Montague Bridge, built by Robert Adam in 1792. Meander along miles of way-marked footpaths, through woodland and along the North or South Esk rivers.

Take a look at Dalkeith's famous livestock. Angora Goats luxuriate in the meadows, Highland Cattle, Clydesdale horses and Wild Boar all live here. Dare the high level walkways, the rope slides and the wild-west fort of the Adventure Play area.

All year round, the Countryside Ranger organises walks, talks and special activities for schools on forestry, wildlife, landscape, history and nature.

EAST LOTHIAN

Where the Tyne meets the sea near Dunbar, the little town's most famous conservationist John Muir is remembered in 1,668 acres of Country Park

The River Forth merges with the North Sea along the East Lothian coast and the length between Musselburgh and Torness power-station is famous for bird watching, beaches and golf. From the coast, laid out in swathes of fertile farmland, the land sweeps gently up to the Lammermuir Hills, dotted with villages. East Lothian buildings have a character all their own; chunky stone houses with crow-step gables, vermilion pantiled roofs, little gardens lush with colour all summer long. Cold in winter if the wind's from the north, here Spring comes early. And it's one of the drier parts of Scotland.

Most of the John Muir Country Park is bird sanctuary, but there's car parking and a welcome for walkers at the Dunbar end, where the cliff top walk is great. The countryside, being relatively level, is perfect for cycling, mostly along quiet back roads, a couple of old railways and good off-road sections. A useful Tourist Information map shows routes – and where you can buy bike spares.

Hard-working and imaginative Countryside Rangers, based in the neat little town of Haddington, do guided walks and organise events anywhere from the coast at Longniddry Bents, Gullane and North Berwick, inland to Pencaitland and up to historic Traprain Law. You'll enjoy panoramic overviews of East Lothian exploring with them the 10 mile route along Deuchrie Edge, mostly on grass tracks, with a few steep climbs. For a more intimate look at cliffs, try their Stories in Stone. Investigate the varied countryside on two

Space to fish in peace

old railways; Pencaitland to Crossgatehall or Longniddry to Haddington, or on one of several rights of way following the Tyne. Rangers also run Dog Walkers' Specials, Environmental Orienteering days and Wildcraft sessions. Become a Nature Detective, do Birdwatching for Beginners, try Beach Art, or seek out Woodland Spirits. Go on a family Puddle Guddle, learn Countryside Folklore or Survival Skills like raft-building. Is a Fossil Frolic a granny-party – or something involved with more serious dinosaurs?

And of course, East Lothian is for the birds. Musselburgh Beach, old ash lagoons and the sea wall are particularly busy in winter with all sorts of waders. You might spot Red-Throated Diver, Velvet Scotar, sea ducks or Greenshank. Go up the River Esk and look for Dipper, Kingfisher, Blackcap, Whitethroat or Yellowhammer. Gosford Bay has Red-Breasted Merganser and Skua. At Ferny Ness watch the Gannets diving. Cheerily berried but prickly Buckthorn scrub, growing at Gullane Bents and along the coast, shelters several sorts of Warblers – easier to hear than to see. The plantation at Yellowcraig has Woodpecker and Woodcock, Crossbill and the occasional Snow Bunting on its way through. Barns Ness is great, specially after a strong easterly wind in Spring or autumn, and you can camp near the lighthouse. Top rarities here are Bluethroat and Red-backed Shrike.

Up on the Lammermuirs, search the sky for raptors like Merlin, Hen Harrier and Peregrine Falcon. Woodland shelter belts and watery places like Whiteadder and Hopes Reservoirs also make good hunting grounds for birds.

PENTLAND HILLS REGIONAL PARK

Practise skiing at Hillend, Midlothian's famous dry ski slope

You can see the Pentland Hills on any approach to Edinburgh. Their bulky landscape provides citizens and visitors with great hill walking country less than half an hour from the city centre, and here's where you can practice your winter sports, at Hillend, Midlothian's famous dry ski slope.

Most of this 980 acre Regional Park is in private ownership, farmed, used for military training, game conservation and water extraction. These have created a wide variety of habitats – and inevitably a few conflicts. Reservoirs and rivers like the North Esk and the Water of Leith encourage wildlife, there's lots of heather moorland though only small areas of trees exist. Some locals are keen to have more woodland.

If you can walk these hills regularly, you're in a wonderful position to observe the yearly cycle of farming as well as wild nature. You'll see grouse moor management, lambing, planting and harvest according to the seasons, with wildlife responding instinctively or automatically. Geese and Whooper Swans fly in around October and out again in

April; in December Stoats and Mountain Hares turn white. You'll find an abundance of wildflowers in early summer, and funghi recycling everything in autumn.

Place names are intriguing. Does anyone know who named Lover's Loup, Shearie Knowe, Cushie Syke, Thrushie Dean, Sinkie Syke or Cauldstane Slap? And why?

Hillend machinery

The inventive Pentland Hills Countryside Rangers, based at Boghall Farm, generate some of the best ideas in Scotland. Like the summer 'Drover Bus'; book your place, hop on at any of 8 Edinburgh stops on the first Sunday morning (not too early) of each month. A bus-riding Ranger gives you a map, guide, local knowledge, a weather forecast, helps you plan your day's journey then drops you off. You do your walk, whether a gentle ramble around the reservoirs, a strenuous hike, or a historic trek; like the 7 mile Thieves' Road from Little Vantage, past Baddingsgill Reservoir and down to West Linton. Tougher types might follow the ridges over Scald Law, Carnethy and Turnhouse Hills for 7 miles, climbing to 2,000 feet. Later in the afternoon (but not too late) the bus collects you at one of three friendly pubs, and returns you to Edinburgh. How civilised.

Walkers have eight other Pentland trails to enjoy. Reasonably fit, you'll do Bavelaw to Kitchen Moss in around 4 hours. In 1 hour, try Flotterstone to Castlelaw Farm's iron age fort and souterrain, onwards to Glencorse, or choose the level Harlaw to Black Springs and Threipmuir walk.

Countryside Rangers will also 'make a date' with you on the hills. Try Shepherding on the Edge to see lambing in progress. Investigate 400 million years of geological history, walk the literary landscapes of Robert Louis Stevenson or take a Map and Compass course. Rangers also run issue-based walks where expert opinions open up lively discussion on, for example, conflict between mountain

Pentland bikers

biking (good exercise for humans), erosion and the ecology (problematic for plants). Most events and walks here are free, for some there's a small charge. All ages and levels of ability are catered for and information is on hand at three places – Flotterstone Visitor Centre, Harlaw Ranger Base or Boghall Farm.

Horse riders have limited access and do need to ask permission, but there are ongoing discussions to improve this and a pilot scheme operating at Boghall Farm. Dogs must be kept under close control.

Cyclists are welcome on lower trails where erosion is less of a problem than higher up, and there's a good scary downhill hurtle beside the dry sky slope at Hillend. A useful map indicates which paths you can rattle along freely and which ones carry a high collision risk. Take care on these – crashes with other bikers, horses, dogs and walkers are an ever-increasing hazard. Because some of the trails are remote, you must be able to deal with problems yourself, so go well prepared with food and sensible all-weather clothing. And have fun.

Viaduct on the River Tweed

SOUTH OF SCOTLAND
& THE BORDERS

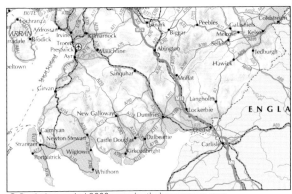

© Bartholomew Ltd 2000 www.bartholomewmaps.com

INFORMATION
OS Map Nos 73–80, 82–84
LOCAL AUTHORITIES
Dumfries and Galloway Council
English Street, Dumfries DG1 2DD
Tel 01387 260000

Scottish Borders Council
Newton St Boswells
Melrose TD6 OSA
Tel 01835 824000

South Ayrshire Council
Wellington Square
Ayr KA7 1DR
Tel 01292 612000

TOURIST INFORMATION CENTRES
Dumfries and Galloway Tourist
Information Tel 01387 253862

Scottish Borders Tourist Board
Murray's Green
JedburghTD8 6BT
Tel 01835 863435 or 863688
Website
http.//www.scot-borders.co.uk

EVENTS LINE FOR THE
BORDERS Tel 01750 20054

Coldstream (Seasonal)
Tel 01890 882607

Eyemouth (Seasonal)
Tel 01890 750678

Galashiels (Seasonal)
Tel 01896 755551

Hawick Tel 01450 372547

Kelso (Seasonal)
Tel 01573 223464

Melrose (Seasonal)
Tel 01896 822555

Peebles Tel 01721 720138

COUNTRYSIDE RANGER SERVICES , COUNTRY PARKS AND ESTATES
Dumfries and Galloway
Countryside Ranger Services
Tel 01387 260184

Harestanes Countryside Rangers
Tel 01835 830281

South Scotland is made for holidays, weekends and days out in the fresh air and some of it is less than an hour's journey from the Central Belt. Come south – and forget crowds. Thousands of people visit the Borders each year but you don't see them because there is simply so much space to enjoy. You can easily fill a fortnight or longer exploring the possibilities here.

This part of Scotland is split from Cumbria's Lake District by the treacherously fascinating Solway Firth and

Harestanes Visitor Centre
(Seasonal) Tel 01835 830306

St Abbes Head
Tel 01890 771443

Bowhill Country Park
Tel 01750 22326

Drumlanrig (Seasonal)
Tel 01848 331555

Traquair (Seasonal)
Tel 01896 830323/785

Thirlstane (Seasonal)
Tel 01578 722430

Grey Mares's Tail (NTS)
NTS Ranger/Naturalist
Tel 01750 42288

Rockcliffe (NTS)
Ranger/Naturalist
Tel 01556 630262

Threave Garden & Estate (NTS)
Ranger/Naturalist
Tel 01556 502575

Hoddom and Kinmount
Tel 01576 300244

Loch Ken
Ranger Tel 01556 502351
Marina Tel 0403 400177 or
01644 470220
Water Ski School
Tel 0705 009 2792

Galloway Forest Park
Tel 01671 402420

Mabie Forest Ranger
Tel 01387 247745

Riks Bikeshed
Tel 01387 270275

Fleet Forest Tel 01556 503626

Dalbeattie Forest
Tel 01556 503626

LONG DISTANCE
ROUTES

Southern Upland Way
Eastern Half Tel 01835 830281
Western Half Tel 01387 260184
website
www.aboutscotland.com/bothy/
suw2.html

St Cuthbert's Way
Tel 01835 830281

North End of Pennine Way
Tel 01835 830281

separated from Northumberland by the deceptively smooth-looking Cheviot Hills and the legendary River Tweed. So you have coastlines, ancient bronze-age forts, rivers, lochs, moors, woodlands and lochs to see. Linked by the Southern Upland Way, the longest Long Distance Footpath in Scotland, the land between Scotland's industrial centre and the English border is full of places to see and interesting things to do. Annual excitements include Gold Panning championships, castle Fairs like those at Drumlanrig and Traquair, galas galore, a festival of jazz at Hawick, an Arts festival at Peebles and of course the famous Common Ridings.

Common Ridings make lively watching and you're welcome to join in the townsfolks' celebrations afterwards, long into the night. Horses are an everyday feature here, so you find horse driving trials, shows and gymkhanas, as well as some of the best riding in Scotland. There are lots of horsey holidays and trekking centres, and amazing B&Bs catering for your steed as well as yourself.

Several Countryside Ranger Services operate. Whether working with local authorities, private estates or NTS, they co-operate to organise events, producing two excellent booklets about these, one for the Scottish Borders and one for Dumfries & Galloway, providing visitors with an easy guide to what's on where. Although agreeing that it's an inexact science, the writers do their best to indicate what level of fitness might be required for each guided walk. You can even take your first tottering steps along sections of the Southern Upland Way with a Countryside Ranger.

On your own, explore castles like Gilnockie Tower, one-time stronghold of border rievers. Rievers could be anything from daring heroes to thieving cattle-rustlers. Seek the shady ruins of tranquil abbeys; this area was popular with the makers of medieval monasteries. Linger long enough and you might even discover who lays flowers on the Lady Devorgilla's tomb in Sweetheart Abbey.

Feeling more active? Then bike the well sign-posted

Four Abbeys Cycle Route. Visit bygone days in great little heritage centres like Carsphairn, and surprise yourself at Gretna Green – it wasn't always about weddings – are they cooking up the Devil's Porridge today? Walk the Raiders' Road, try a Farm Buggy Trail, or seek the ghosts of stolen cattle in the Devil's Beef Tub. Dumfries itself is good for all sorts of museums, from aviation to costume – and witchcraft. Search for the strange stones of Kirkmadrine. Climb the Leadhills – and find gold.

Walk or cycle the south of Scotland woodlands. There's Dalbeattie Forest, Ae Forest, the oakwoods of Fleet Forest with its two-mile interpretative trail, Mabie Forest and Galloway Forest Park. You can fish in lochs and rivers – indeed it won't necessarily break your bank to fish the legendary Tweed itself.

Little towns full of character are dotted throughout; Dumfries, Castle Douglas, Moffat, Melrose, Jedburgh, Kelso, Haddington. Peebles is a good centre – and don't miss scary Neidpath Castle. Pretty villages like St John's Town of Dalry, or Cockburnspath, coastal gems like Rockcliffe, Kippford, Portpatrick and Isle of Whithorn are there for the visiting. The fishing harbours of St Abbs and Eyemouth are worthy of their fame – St Abbs so pretty, Eyemouth so busy and, on a sunny afternoon, treat yourself to tiny Cove, tucked beneath its rose-pink cliff.

Lighthouses and dizzy cliff-walks surround both coasts; you'll teeter along a few at each end of the Southern Upland Way. Corsewall lighthouse has even been turned into a posh hotel. Big headlands around the coast are great places for bird-watching. Try St Abb's Head, or the Mull of Galloway.

One of the best things in the Borders must be its early-September Festival of Walking, when, whatever your age or level of fitness, you'll find a suitable expedition, in the company of knowledgeable and experienced guides.

Literary landscapes to browse through include Robert Burns' Dumfriesshire and John Buchan's Broughton. James

OTHER USEFUL ORGANISATIONS

Scottish Natural Heritage Dumfries & Galloway Area Office Tel 01387 247010

Wildfowl and Wetlands Trust Tel 01387 770200

Mull of Galloway RSPB (Seasonal) Tel 01671 402861

Mersehead Nature Reserve Tel 01387 780298

Ellisland Farm (Seasonal) Tel 01387 740426

Scottish Border Trails at Peebles Tel 01721 720336

PUBLIC TRANSPORT

SCOTRAIL Tel 0345 484950

BUSES

Scottish Borders Rail/Bus Link Tel 01835 825123

Borders Tel 01835 824000

Dumfries and Galloway Tel 0345 090510 (local rate)

MacEwans Coach Services, Dumfries Tel 01387 710357

Walter Scott's view of the
Eildon Hills

Hogg 'the Ettrick Shepherd' loved St
Mary's Loch – and Tibbie Shiels inn
there, while the magical Eildons inspired
Walter Scott – and were the subject of
spooky rumours about wizards. Arty landscapes include the
Moniaive idyll of James Paterson, where there's a neat little
museum about him. Paterson painted the local countryside
walked by 'bonnie Annie Laurie' of the song.

Cross your palm with cabbage and what do you get?
Answer, visit outposts of Edinburgh's Royal Botanic Garden;
Dawyck for conifers, flowering trees and rhododendrons,
Logan for tree ferns and cabbage palms. And NTS's Threave
Garden has its own Countryside Ranger Service to guide
you around.

Nature Reserves are everywhere. Listen for Pied
Flycatchers or Redstarts in the ancient Wood of Cree, slosh

Melrose Abbey

through the saltmarshes of Mersehead,
catch up with migrating waterfowl at
Caerlaverock or Castlehead. Of course
you might prefer to dream away the
sunny summer hours on one of the many
sandy beaches, thinking of what you
might do if only you had the energy . . .
But first, take a look at the following
temptations.

BERWICKSHIRE & THE SOUTH-EAST

The south-eastern corner of Scotland is all rolling hills, well-kept farmland and plushy estates, threaded together by one of Scotland's greatest rivers, the Tweed. The coastline is made of bulky headlands and cliffs, little bays and fishing harbours. Because the Borders are famous for pheasant shooting, salmon fishing and farming you might think there wouldn't be much of a welcome for visitors, but in fact an increasing mileage of good walking and cycling routes have been mutually agreed, and made accessible to everyone, by landowners and local authorities.

The Tweed Cycleway crosses Scotland from Carstairs to Berwick, Sustrans no 1 National Cycle Route should be passing through by 2005, and an excellent booklet details twenty trails, from easy to demanding – and shows where you can buy spare parts. Meander along quiet back roads and disused railways, choose multi-day trips, off-road forest tracks, or go mountain bike racing at Innerleithen. Take the family from Harestanes to the Minto Hills, choosing the 7 mile route. If you're fitter do the full 16 miles, or head out the 20 miles to Kelso.

Scottish Borders Council Countryside Rangers, based at Harestanes Countryside Centre, have info on local bird-watching and walking clubs, the Borders Wildlife Watch Clubs for 8-12s, and how to volunteer your services for the good of the environment. They take guided walks around the district in all seasons; travelling all sorts of habitats from

North Sea landscape

the North Sea coast up the Tweed and Teviot valleys, revealing local secrets of nature, geology and history. In co-operation with various other agencies they offer you an astonishing variety of informative booklets and maps. There's a compact, comprehensive events programme too; tramp in the footsteps of Roman legions, make a pilgrimage along St Cuthbert's Way, cycle the Four Abbeys Way, or stretch your legs up to panoramic Peniel Heugh, once the fastness of a Celtic tribe.

You can cross from England into Scotland along the north end of the 250 mile-long Pennine Way – on the low-level or the high-level route up to Kirk Yetholm, following the Border Ridge, with splendid views in good weather.

Southern Upland Way near Melrose

St Cuthbert's Way is 62 miles of varied walking between Melrose and the island of Lindisfarne where, planning your journey to coincide with the tides, you walk the Lindisfarne causeway. The route takes you up onto the Eildon Hills, along Roman Dere Street to Harestanes, past mighty Cessford Castle, once guardian of the route you're following over the hills and across the English border into Northumberland. Pause to consider St Cuthbert's Cave on your way out to the coastal Nature Reserve. Easy riverside lengths alternate with more strenuous hilly stretches, all way-marked but you need to know how to navigate, and take all-weather gear. Lots of this route goes through private land – plan where you're going to overnight as camping is not an option. Who was Cuthbert? A Prior of Lindisfarne who

Eyemouth Harbour and walkers

started in Melrose around 650 AD. Melrose has its own supply of Tweed folk who earn their permit money by instructing those of us who'd like to learn how to catch fish. And a permit to fish trout there can be had for under £20.

The 18 mile-long stretch of the Borders Abbeys Way walks you past one of the best salmon beats of the Tweed from Kelso Abbey, crosses interesting bridges, the oldest dating from 1795, passes the crumbled remains of 12th century Roxburgh Castle, goes on up the Teviot and takes off up Jed Water to Jedburgh Abbey. Parts of this walk are good for bird life; Moorhens, Mute Swans, Oystercatchers and perhaps a Heron. History buffs will enjoy Roxburgh village's gravestones, 16th century Wallace's Tower, stronghold of the Kers, and John Miller's Victorian railway viaduct. You'll pass caves where Bonnie Prince Charlie's horses hid in 1745. You'll also pass a few strategically placed tearooms, TICs and bus stops. Extending the route to include Melrose and Dryburgh Abbey, Hawick and Selkirk brings you up to 65 miles.

Harestanes is worth a visit. Open all summer, originally

the estate farm steading, it houses a shop, tea-room, loos, traditional craft demonstrations, and a nearby car park. The ground floor, courtyard, picnic tables and wildlife garden are good for people with wheelchairs. For youngsters there's a Play Area and very sensible Games and Discovery Rooms. Not far away, Jed Forest Deer Park runs a children's nature club. Your dog can go too, but only on a lead, for this is farming country. Your leaflet will remind you that plants need their flowers for survival, so please to leave them unpicked.

St Abbs Head and village

Out on the edge of Berwickshire, inhale the sea air at Coldingham and the fishing harbours of Eyemouth and St Abbs. Walk the Town Trail at Eyemouth and watch the fishing fleet unloading its cargo. Follow the coastline along cliff-top paths, see Hairy Ness, Gallow's Law, head for Hurker's Haven and Breeches Rock on your way to Burnmouth, or shiver your spine at Fast Castle – False Castle – a gaunt ruin where local wreckers once tempted ships to their doom for the sake of their cargo.

St Abbs Head is where you'll see Kittiwakes, Razorbills and Guillemots galore. If you're a diver, you'll find soul-mates at St Abbs village.

The September Festival of Walking is a week-long celebration of the countryside, when you can explore the Borders from a different venue each year. Walks are graded Easy, Moderate to Strenuous; easy might be along the riverbanks or the shore, strenuous a 14 mile hill climb. The week ends with a Grand Ceilidh. What fun.

Bowhill toadstool

BUCCLEUCH ESTATES

Bowhill and the Buccleuch estates cover huge areas of the Scottish Borders, including their satellites Dalkeith and Drumlanrig Castle. For around five months every summer everyone's welcome and during the rest of the year there's a policy of open access for walkers. Because of its location in Midlothian, Dalkeith Country Park is included in the Edinburgh & the Lothians section. Based within Buccleuch Country Parks, Countryside Rangers take guided walks there and in the surrounding areas.

Lovely Bowhill, mentioned affectionately in Scott's *Lay of the Last Minstrel*, lies between the valleys of the Ettrick and the Yarrow. Miles of way-marked trails lead you through mature woodlands, around peaceful lochs and alongside rivers. Bowhill courtyard is a good place to begin, with the Ranger's office, a great exhibition about the estate's plants and wildlife, a café, shop and loos. Not far away the kids can tackle the adventure playground with its aerial ropeways and giant slides, and everyone can picnic. Try the August

Bowhill wildlife exhibition – fox

Activity Week, with Pond Dipping, a Minibeast Safari, sessions on Woodland Wildlife, a Treasure Trail and a Family Orienteering day. Year about, at Bowhill and Drumlanrig, Open Days help you discover how these estates tick, with tree-felling and planting demonstrations and other relevant activities.

Bowhill Estate is the natural choice for horse riders

Bowhill Countryside Ranger is very child-friendly, arranging school Treasure Hunts, expeditions for packs of Guides and Brownies, running the monthly Watch group for young wildlife enthusiasts and using her arty craft skills to update displays in the courtyard exhibition.

You'll find leaflets on self-guided, way-marked trails, like the level 2 mile Loch Walk which gives you a chance to watch fishing – or the Moorhens, Goldeneyes and Swans. Explore the Duchess's Drive, a 7 mile hike over the moors and far away, following a Victorian carriage route through history and spectacular scenery. Venture through Black Andrew Wood, see 15th century Newark Castle – once a royal hunting lodge – and pass Pernassie Hill's remnants of the old Ettrick forest, once a king's hunting ground. This walk takes at least three and a half hours. On another, meet the Three Brethren, following the idyllic Yarrow Water into the hills. Or find Slain Men's Lead on the 3 mile Lady's Walk. On any of these you might spot Roe deer, Red Squirrels, Hedgehogs, Chiff-chaffs, Tree Creepers or Wrens. Many species of plant grow freely here. Look for Queen of the Meadow, Wild Strawberry, Self Heal, Violets, Woodrush and Bluebells.

The fascination at Bowhill is in its woodlands. Since the 17th century, thoughtful planting and tree conservation down the generations to the present day has made the estate world famous for its integrated land management. Each

Fishing on the loch at
Bowhill Estate

winter it decorates Edinburgh with huge Christmas trees.

This estate is a natural choice for riders. You can bring your horse here for long rides, staying in local B&Bs with stabling. There's a 57 mile way-marked and mapped Equestrian Route taking around 3–4 days to complete, a pilot scheme to see if riders will enjoy such a facility. Best between April and October, so you're not shot or tree-felled over, there's even an optional taxi service to transport your gear.

At Drumlanrig Castle Country Park you can hire bikes and try out the trails – there's even a cycle museum. The Douglas stronghold of yore, it's now a pleasant estate of hills and valleys open to all. Ranger-led walks take you through the wildlife and history, craft workshops happen, most days you'll see bird of prey demonstrations, and you'll find an adventure playground, shop, tearoom and loos. People in wheelchairs can get around here. In all Buccleuch parks, dogs are welcome on leads.

The start of the Southern
Upland Way at the village of
Cockburnspath

THE SOUTHERN UPLAND WAY

Spanning 212 miles from east to west, the Southern Upland Way is Scotland's most demanding Long Distance Footpath. The longest and therefore perhaps the most satisfying to complete, this route is neither for the faint-hearted nor the unfit.

Yet, while there are long hard slogs over seemingly endless moor, there are pretty bits too, and you do go through wonderfully remote areas that are never seen by road users. The air is full of heathery mossy smells and the only sounds are the calls of Whaups and Peewits, the sough of the wind and the bleating of sheep. Apart, that is, from the daily heart-stopping scream of RAF bombers. Sundays are quieter.

You do need to be a strong, experienced hill walker to do the Way in a oner. It takes between 10 and 20 days. However, many visitors from afar opt to tackle it a section at a time, returning year on year till they've done the lot. People from nearer do short stretches each weekend, some 'collecting' these till they've walked whole Way, others preferring to repeat favourite stretches. The official guide details 15 manageable sections and the Rangers' leaflets show some shorter circular routes connected with the Way.

Whatever strategy you choose, you'll find some great spots on the journey – smugglers' coves, secret hamlets, unknown lochs and memorials to long forgotten Scots, under wider, bigger skyscapes than you've ever imagined. The

The statue of Borders writer James Hogg 'the Ettrick Shepherd' looks over Tibbie Shiels Inn and St Mary's Loch

weather too may give you more variety than you bargained for.

If you want to start with your toes in the actual North Sea, look for a tunnel through the cliff, follow it down and paddle in tiny Cove harbour, once a handy haunt for smugglers. Pretty villages on your westward journey will include Cockburnspath, Abbey St Bathans, Longformacus and Fairnilee. Wanlockhead reputedly has gold in them thar hills to take your mind off your blistered feet. Sanquar follows and, a long way later there's St John's Town of Dalry and New Luce.

Crossing the River Tweed at Melrose

Innerleithen and Traquair have welcoming hostelries. Romantic Traquair has the oldest continually inhabited house in Scotland, where, 800 years ago Alexander I signed a charter, where the Stuarts supported Mary Queen of Scots and the Jacobites and where the enchanted woods and secret stairways have been inspiring novelists since Walter Scott. 27 monarchs have visited Traquair before you – and you might see one of the ghosts.

You'll cross pretty upland burns and several major rivers, you'll skirt big stretches of water like Watch Water reservoir, St Mary's Loch, Daer Reservoir and Clatteringshaws. Spare energy? Climb various heights along the Way, like

A walker at St John's Town of Dalry

Lowther Hill, 2379 ft. You'll pass through coniferous forest continously being harvested and replanted, more with the walker in mind than previously. Among the conifers you might see special birds like Siskins, Short Eared Owls, and the purpose-built Crossbills who skilfully tweak seeds out of pine cones. Wheatears come from Africa for the summer.

You'll also pass through decidous woodland, follow ancient drove roads, go over passes, come across ruined cottages and castles. Interesting stopping places are scattered somewhat unevenly; Lauder is friendly, and you can camp at nearby Thirlestane Castle, a 16th century improvement of a 13th century stronghold, complete with tearoom, shop and loos. Melrose is a favourite watering hole, with lots to see and do while you're there, from its Abbey to its little Wynd Theatre and cheery pubs. Bustling Galashiels is nearby and Beattock is near Moffat, a lively wee town with big welcomes for visitors.

Two Countryside Ranger Services look after the Way, one based at Harestanes, one in Dumfries. With their guidance you can walk sections, finding out about the geology, history and wildlife around – an excellent introduction. The route passes through most of the habitat types of southern Scotland, so you have a good chance of seeing a sample of everything that lives and breathes there at the particular time of year at which you've chosen to walk. It's worth contacting the Rangers before you set out, for any useful up-to-date information. TICs have maps and

The steps at the western end of the Way to the bay at Portpatrick

useful info sheets about accommodation, transport, and guides.

Because most of the Way goes over land used for domestic animals you're asked to leave your dogs at home. Console yourself with the sight of Belted Galloway cattle and Blackface sheep. The Way being for walkers, it's unsuitable for horses or bikes.

May and June are best for wildflowers and birdsong, but any time from April to the end of September can be good along the Southern Upland Way. Winter walking is perfectly possible and can be brilliant on sparklingly clear frosty days, however always be well prepared for howling gales and driving sleet, for there's little shelter.

The route is way-marked, but you'll need to know how to navigate with a map and compass when the visibility is bad. You'll need good all-weather equipment and you must be resourceful enough to handle emergencies yourself.

Castle Kennedy is worth a visit as you head west, with its lovely gardens. Finally you tiptoe along western cliff tops through drifts of sea pinks and butterflies till you totter down neatly made steps and fling your weary boots triumphantly into Portpatrick harbour at your journey's end, where warm-hearted hostelries line the side of this busy little fishing port, just waiting to welcome you.

Threave's 1,497 acre estate has agriculture, forestry and nature conservation working in harmony. The Stable courtyard makes a comprehensive Countryside Centre

THREAVE GARDENS

Threave Gardens is at the centre of a trio of NTS properties in south west Scotland, each very different from the others. Whilst Threave is gloriously pretty and full of unusual cultivated plants and trees, the Grey Mare's Tail is all dramatic scenery, scary heights and frisky waterfall. Rockcliff is a little smiley bay with a wondrous collection of rock pools and bird life. A woodland footpath winds round the coast to Kippford. There's a programme of guided walks around all of these throughout the summer.

Threave is worth a visit any time of year, with 64 acres of garden spectacularly clad in 200 varieties of daffodil in spring, its herbaceous borders gloriously colourful all summer and its mature trees and heathers a riot of reds and golds in autumn. The Visitor Centre itself is open Easter to late October. But there are also things to do here, and a Countryside Ranger service to help. All these trees and bushes encourage a good variety of wildlife, especially birds, and the wetlands encourage over-wintering wildfowl, wading birds and special plants. Watch them from strategically placed hides, explore further afield on a 2 mile trail which samples several landscape types – or take a class in amateur gardening. For people with disabilities there are wheelchairs and an electric battery car to help you reach most of the interesting places along smooth paths, like the walled garden, the visitor centre, restaurant and shop.

There are no visitor facilities at the Grey Mare's Tail, which looks exactly like its name – a 200 ft fall of water between two steeply rounded hills. Spectacular rather than beautiful, famous for having sheltered 17th century Covenanters, and for having lost Sir Walter Scott in a fog, it is actually quite dangerous to visit – there have been several fatal accidents. However, the able-bodied can admire it safely enough from the paths leading up from the car park and there's a remote control video camera to help your bird watching. The 2,279 acres of NTS land extending to Loch Skeen, White Coomb and Dob's Linn gives you lots of scope for walking and enjoying an unusual variety of wildflowers. All summer you can go on Ranger-guided walks. The geology is interesting, and you might even see the herd of wild goats. Nearby Moffat has all the facilities you might need to keep body and soul together.

Admire the view from Rockcliffe village

Around Rockcliffe you can skiddle on the beach, explore dozens of fascinating rock pools, or take your imagination back in time on its ancient 20 acre hill fort The Mote of Mark. Also 20 acres, Rough Island is an offshore bird sanctuary but don't go while they're nesting in May and June. Between Rockcliffe and Kippford lie the Muckle Lands, where you can walk the Jubilee Path either way for a completely idyllic experience in summer, with gusts of fresh air and lovely views all year round. Rockcliffe village has good car parking, a tearoom, shop, loos, and seats thoughtfully placed around the bay.

With the NTS Countryside Ranger/Naturalist you might opt for a Fossil Foray in the Moffat valley, search for the source of the Grey Mare's Tail river, test your tastebuds on Nature's Harvest or learn some Secrets of the Seashore at Rockcliffe, walk out to Rough Island when the tide's right, go birdwatching there, or discover whether Robert the Bruce was a likely 'twitcher' at Lochmaben Castle. You might do a session on trees or wildflowers of the coast or hills, spend a Springtime afternoon Meeting the Mammals of Threave – or enjoy a Fathers' Day Ramble.

photo: Andrew Morris

The statue of Scotland's
national poet, Robert Burns in
Dumfries.
Robert Burns spent his last
years in Dumfries and you can
walk along the river at Ellisland,
his farm

DUMFRIESSHIRE
& THE SOUTH WEST

Dumfries & Galloway include some of the most welcoming places in Scotland, with enough happening to keep anyone actively occupied for weeks on end. Accessible hills, forests and lochs, farmland, hidden byways and quiet roads lead you on journeys of exploration, tempting you onward to discover yet more. Clean air warmed by the Gulf Stream fills your lungs and there's hardly any traffic. The air is so unpolluted that at night the stars look close enough to touch.

Medieval raids, kidnappings, blackmail and murder, have left the Solway coast stuffed with castles for you to visit. Try the fortress of Caerlaverock, and a Rievers' Trail to help your imagination take you back in time. Archaeology and history feature strongly, from cave-dwellers to 5th century Whithorn, the first Christian church in Scotland. Robert the Bruce went there on pilgrimages. Robert Burns spent his last years around Dumfries and you can walk along the river at Ellisland, his farm.

No fewer than 18 organisations provide guided walks. Hoddom and Kinmount Estates operate a summer ranger service, the Farming and Wildlife Advisory Group run a National Farm Walk week plus evening walks, or you can try a Wildlife Safari with the Wildfowl & Wetlands Trust. Dumfries & Galloway Council Countryside Rangers run a full programme of events in co-operation with many of these so, on your visit, you can learn Heather Management using Blackface Sheep, experience Natterjack Nights, World Ocean Day, enter Carlingwark Loch Rowing Competition, go on a Big Yeuchy Mud Walk – or a hunt the Headless Horseman up Tynron Doon.

Apart from the Southern Upland Way, which passes through, there are hundreds of miles of local footpaths and cycle trails to explore. Take a Walk on the Wildside at the 'Muckle Toon' of Langholm, one-time scene of the Battle of Arkinhome (1455). Try a half-hour Duchess Bridge Walk looking for Dippers along the idyllic River Esk, or test your level of fitness doing the longer and more strenuous Monumental Mini Hike up Whita Hill. There's good town walking in arty Kirkcudbright with its little harbour – and

Rik's Bike Shed, Mabie

nearby beaches to laze about on afterwards. Further west, try some of the five recommended walks around Castle Douglas; ranging from easy to strenuous, they'll take you to Threave Castle, around Carlingwark Loch with a boardwalk to help you, and over Cuckoo Bridge. You'll come across well-placed bird hides on the way.

Galloway Forest Park is Britain's largest at 300 square miles big. Mabie's friendly Forest Rangers run year-round events like woodland 'Spring Cleans', Wildflower Wanders, and brilliant Den-building woodcraft and tracking afternoons – about survival in the forest. In December, Mabie Fayre is all fun and festivities – buy your Christmas tree, craft works and gifts. Mabie has walks, with routes for horse riders, but really specialises in big mountain bike trails. Catch some air on 'the Full Mental' week end biking course, dancing the nights away, at Rik's Bike Shed.

Glen Trool Visitor Centre, Kirroughtree Visitor Centre, Clatteringshaws Wildlife Centre (open all summer) have cafés, loos, and are also start points for way-marked cycle routes.

Horsey? You'll find at least half a dozen pony trekking or horse riding centres. Keen on freshwater? Loch Ken is 9 miles of mixed recreation; coarse fishing and water sports from canoeing to windsurfing and waterskiing. Up in the Ken-Dee Marshes Nature Reserve you might come across overwintering Greenland Whitefronted Geese.

Although the Mull of Galloway is a long way from anywhere, this most southerly point of Scotland has prehistoric fortifications, a lighthouse and a bird sanctuary. Nearer Ireland and the Isle of Man than anywhere else, most days you can see both clearly. Corsewall Point gives you great views up the Clyde and you can always call into the neat lighthouse hotel for some hospitality.

Mersehead's wet meadows, salt marshes and mudflats attract a great variety of winter wildfowl. Walking the quiet Machars – low-lying land between Glenluce, Isle of Whithorn and Wigtown – gives you lots of scope not only for bird watching, but also for sheer atmosphere. Ancient peoples left more than their mark here and you can see why film makers chose this area to make *The Wicker Man*. There's plenty of evidence of early human habitation left, in 6,000 year-old flint artefacts, prehistoric stone circles like Torhouse – and place names. Maybe two millennia of Christianity show at St Ninian's Cave, Whithorn Priory, Glenluce Abbey and the Martyrs' Stake, and a Victorian fisherman once hooked a Roman cooking pot out of Carlinwark Loch, but who named Cruggleton? Drochtag? Gleds Nest? Screel Hill? The Castle of Sinniness? Mosses like Derskelpin, Knocketie, Annabaglish and Mindork, the Flow of Airriequhillart? Does Glen Luce mean the valley of light – or the lewd place? And where's that crannog gone?

While livestock farming has created fields, farms and neat villages, there's still plenty of room for wildlife. This is the only part of Scotland where you might find Natterjack Toads, rare fish like the Sparling and unusual plants like Whorled Caraway. Skeins of Barnacle Geese fly in over the Solway Flats, Peregrine Falcons and Golden Eagles swoop and dive above the hills of Galloway Forest Park.

Five major salmon rivers flow from the hills, you might catch sea-trout, and the burns and lochs are good for both native 'brownies' and stocked Rainbow Trout. There's deer stalking, wild goat, pheasant, grouse, partridge or wild goose shooting on the big estates or the Solway marshes.

And if by chance you do have bad weather? Head for Scotland's only book town, Wigtown. You see? This part of Scotland has . . . well . . . it simply has everything.

Castle Loch, Lochmaben

OUTLOOK

What responsibilities do we urban freedom-seekers have, stravaiging about on land that is someone else's bread and butter? Land access issues have to be tackled always with care. Whose rights are more important – those of us who need fresh air to help us survive urban pressures, or those who strive to scrape a living from the land? And further conflicts arise; who has the right to a particular path – walkers or bikers? Dog-walkers or toddlers? Galloping horses or wheelchair users? It is heartening to see how, with goodwill, diplomacy and co-operation on all sides, ways are being found to resolve these difficulties.

We have other problems to solve. Country Parks designated for public use vary widely in quality. Many have wonderfully equipped Visitor Centres and networks of usable paths, a few lack even the most basic necessities. Most Countryside Rangers welcome visitors, a few believe their mission is to protect our landscape from humans, actively discouraging access. Too many visitor centres close between October and April; users would like to see them open and manned, at least over weekends and school holidays. They'd like to know there's an expert on hand, for information and guidance, and they'd like unlocked toilets.

There is also the question of health and safety in Country Parks designated for everyone's use. If there's a scary bit of yours, get together with other locals to reclaim it, and make a fuss till you get some form of policing or the regular presence of wardens there. We should tolerate no no-go areas in our parks.

Finally, we need to invest in greater numbers of Countryside Rangers. Lone Rangers have too much to do; they can't be manning an office, rebuilding a path, monitoring migrating geese and leading a guided walk at the same time – yet an empty visitor centre is of little use to anyone and no answering machine can adequately reply to questions about terrain, weather and facilities.

But future prospects look good. Whatever the detail of the new land legislation, with mutual respect and understanding of each others' problems access to the countryside should continue to improve.

BEING OUT THERE SAFELY

PREPARATION

Strap on a day-sack containing spare layers of dry clothing, socks, waterproofs, any local information leaflets, a map, compass, whistle, food and drink and a basic first aid kit.

Plan your outing.

Travel within your capabilities.

THE COUNTRY CODE

Make no unnecessary noise

Do not start fires

Keep to the paths

Use gates and stiles to avoid damage to fences, hedges and walls

Leave gates as you find them

Keep dogs under control

Take your litter home

Keep all water clean

Protect wildlife, wild plants and trees

Go carefully on country roads

Leave livestock, crops and machinery alone

TAKE NOTHING BUT PICTURES,
LEAVE NOTHING BUT FOOTPRINTS

BE WATER WISE

SPOT THE DANGERS: water can look safe, but be dangerous. Learn to spot and keep away from dangers

KNOW THE DIFFERENCE: You may be able to swim in a warm indoor pool, but that does not mean you will be able to cope in cold outdoor water

CHECK NEW PLACES: They may have hidden dangers. Always ask somebody who knows

MOBILE PHONE

Can be a useful extra, but can not be relied on to get you out of trouble anywhere in the Scottish hills, where there is almost no service.

Don't phone for help unless you're in a really bad way.